THE FIELD OF BEING

Also by Don C. Nix

Loss of Being

.

THE FIELD OF BEING

✦

Collected Thoughts on The Unfolding Evolution of Consciousness

Don C. Nix, J.D., Ph.D.

iUniverse, Inc.
New York   Bloomington

The Field of Being

Collected Thoughts on the Evolution of Human Consciousness

iUniverse books may be ordered through booksellers or by contacting:

iUniverse
1663 Liberty Drive
Bloomington, IN 47403
www.iuniverse.com
1-800-Authors (1-800-288-4677)

ISBN: 978-1-4401-4319-9 (pbk)
ISBN: 978-1-4401-4320-5 (ebk)

Printed in the United States of America

iUniverse rev. date: 5/7/2009

Dedication

With gratitude to Ann Fursman Nix, my wife, my lover, my best friend, my best critic, my soul-task partner, the source of countless deep insights, and the other end of a non-stop conversation for the last 53 years, still going strong and showing no signs of abating. With great love and appreciation.

Don C. Nix
Sonoma, CA
May, 2009

Contents

Introduction

In our time, the discoveries of quantum physics are folding back to meet the expressions of the ancient Wisdom Traditions. Our understanding of reality, propounded by Rene Descartes and Isaac Newton, and assumed to be eternally valid, is dissolving into something new and mysterious. While the earlier reality involved an assemblage of independent, material parts existing in a stable, static universe of empty space, the new emerging reality is neither stable nor static. It is a universe of probabilities rather than predictable cause and effect. It functions less like a machine and more like a dynamic web of interpenetrating things and events. Space itself is not empty but a plenum, filled with seething subatomic particles. Material forms and light are merging into one. This reality is not yet fully in place.

The new view was presaged with some accuracy in the Chinese Avatamsaka Sutra of some 1,700 years ago, rephrased recently by Sir Charles Eliot:

In the heaven of Indra, there is said to be a network of pearls, so arranged that if you look at one you see all the others reflected in it. In the same way each object in the world is not merely itself but involves every other object and in fact is everything else. In every particle of dust, there are present Buddhas without number.

One of the major benefits of this massive shift in understanding is the possibility that the split between spiritual reality and scientific reality may be moving towards healing. The two bodies of thought share a goal of attempting to understand the reality of the universe. After 400 years of polarization, the two appear now to be converging. Among the disturbing trends of our world, this is one that is profoundly encouraging.

1

Our Lineage

We are stardust,
blown through infinities
of living night,
to this lovely, green little
planet,
to dance the dream of life,
and to undertake the task
of stardust
everywhere:
to shine,
to shine,
to shine.

We are, quite literally, stardust. Our personal biography begins 13.7 billion years ago with the Big Bang. It continues through the swirling creation of billions of galaxies. Some of the stars in those galaxies exploded in spectacular cataclysm, creating carbon atoms that found their way to Earth and eventually became our bodies. Starbursts are the only way that carbon is created in the universe. We are the progeny of exploding stars. And, we are the Earth. We are more than connected to the Earth. We are the Earth. We are made of the Earth. We are that part of the Earth that gets up and walks around on itself. We are each a pool of pure, living consciousness that has picked up a little earth, a little cosmic dust, to form a body around it.

The stardust image is also apt because science is telling us these days that we are beings of light. It recently became possible to actually measure the light emitted by a human being. Wisdom traditions all over the Earth have talked in these terms for thousands of years. We are beginning to realize that we are beings of living light and consciousness that have a body as an appendage or attachment. We are temporary whirlpools of livingness, light, energy, awareness and intelligence--surrounded by a vast ocean, a cosmic Field of livingness, light, energy, awareness and intelligence. When our personal whirlpool stops, we melt back into that ocean. We were never separate from it. We were only temporarily organized into a small whirlpool in this living cosmic ocean. What this means is that we can never fall out of this vast ocean of life. We can only melt back into it. We can only go home to this cosmic Field of livingness, which abides miraculously, infinitely, and eternally.

2

A Leap in Evolution

I carry life like a tide,
with ebbs and flows,
and sustaining power.
I am the heart of innovation,
and I am the soul of destruction.
The grasses grow in me,
the blood flows in me,
the heart beats in me,
the mind thinks in me,
the eye sees in me,
the ear hears in me.
I make life beautiful,
I make life meaningful,
I make life move.
Wake up to me.
Open up to me.
and join my celebration.

The things of the material world emerge mysteriously forth from Unmanifest Being into this three-dimensional realm of matter where we live. Once they reach the material level, they begin a ceaseless process of metamorphosis. The dictionary defines metamorphosis as change that occurs from within. This describes what is happening to every object in the material world. We sometimes call this metamorphosis evolution. In the latter stages, we may call it erosion. In the human being, we call it aging. Everything in the material realm is undergoing perpetual change, which ends with the disappearance of the object back into the ocean of Being.

In its guise as evolution, metamorphosis has over millennia taken the human species from primates in the trees to ourselves. We are a kaleidoscope of changing forms through time. We walk around today as the latest model of this long process. As a result of Darwin's work, we tend to think of evolution in physical terms, but our consciousness and our awareness of reality have also been steadily evolving.

In the present moment, we may be witnessing a leap in the evolution of our consciousness. Perhaps the speedup is due to the threat that we have posed to ourselves. We appear to be in a race with time to mature and evolve quickly enough to avoid destroying our world and destroying ourselves. Our choice is to evolve or die. Nothing so wonderfully concentrates the mind as the threat of annihilation. This pressure encourages an evolutionary leap, or hyper-evolution. We are threatened by our own success, our own inventions, and a regressed worldview of ourselves as separate and self-interested entities. We need to make a leap in consciousness that is as great as the leap from simple animal consciousness to human self-consciousness. The leap required now is from self-consciousness to what may be termed Field consciousness—the realization, held consciously and sustained throughout everyday life—of our unity with the Cosmos and all its inhabitants. We may appear to be separate entities, but at the level of our ground we are all just one thing—Pure Being, or the universe. With Field consciousness in place, we could operate in a state of "Inter-Being"—awareness of the fact that we are merged with and woven into all other life-forms. The perspective of separate self-interest leads inevitably to exploitation of others and Earth's resources, which is a formula for creeping disaster, as we now see all around us. With Field consciousness, we would not exploit our fellows for our own gain. We would not trash our world. We would pay attention to the plight of others as well as our own because their interest would be our interest. In a humanity aware of the singularity of the cosmos, that would be the operating principle in our life.

There is some hope that we can accomplish this necessary evolution. All over the world, more and more of us are waking up and experiencing our oneness, not only with each other, but with nature and with the Cosmos. More and more of us are experiencing what Levy-Bruhl called "Participation Mystique," the experience of merging with Being and the livingness of the natural world. Participation mystique carries with it a sense of sacredness and wonder. It contains a sense of connection. It widens our perceptual screen and makes it large enough to include all other humans, including future generations, all other life-forms, and the planet itself, which sustains our life. The Sufis call this state of merged consciousness "Sa'ada," which means "Nearness to Being."

So, our survival depends on our ability to evolve from the old mode of consciousness—with its worldview based on separate self-interest—to a new worldview centered on the unity and commonality of the Field. This is a tall order, given the time pressure created by the present march toward disaster, and the fact that we must change the consciousness of literally billions of people. However, there are precedents.

In 1565, when Copernicus issued his reality-shattering theory that the earth moved around the sun, no-one agreed with his view. In 1610, Galileo restated the Copernican thesis, and was forced by the Catholic Church to recant his heliocentric theory. For his beliefs, he spent the rest of his life under house arrest by the Roman Inquisition. One hundred years later, this view was the accepted reality throughout the Western world. The leap in worldview spread quickly because the world was primed and ready for it, and because it was the verifiable truth. Today, having reaped the whirlwind of separate self-interest for several millennia, we are yearning for another possibility. We can hope that, as a species, we are primed and ready for a leap in consciousness to the worldview of unity. We need to evolve now, in some haste, into another great truth.

3

The Dying Worldview

A lonely withering leaf,
having lost its affray with the wind,
releases its grip on the tree,
and falls.
Recently proudly green,
now browned by the shadow of time,
it returns to the dust of the earth,
color-first.

Everything in the material world eventually wears out and disappears back into the ocean of Being that originally threw it forth. The pattern of the unfolding is familiar. The object emerges from Being fresh and bursting with life-force. It grows and develops, comes into its full maturity, erodes and begins to disintegrate, and finally, worn out, disappears. Its disappearance opens a space and a possibility for new life to emerge.

This template of creation, metamorphosis and destruction applies throughout the universe at the material level. Cells, humans, trees, mountains, planets, stars and galaxies are all temporary, though the time scale may range from brief to vast.

Civilizations also come and go, as history demonstrates.

The cultural complex of a civilization is the set of beliefs, assumptions and perceptions that are shared, at both conscious and unconscious levels, by its people. It determines what is accepted, largely unquestioned, as reality. It is the culture's worldview, into which children are, generation after generation, initiated and educated. The cultural complex extends over time, providing common assumptions about life and reality that serve to bind the people together.

The worldview is subject to the same cycle of deterioration and renewal that we observe in the realm of material objects. Societies change. Beliefs change as societies change, and societies change as beliefs change. Perceptions of reality evolve at the individual level and at the level of society. Today, we are on the cusp of a massive shift in our worldview. Our old worldview is out-dated and exhausted. It is ripe for renewal. That worldview, which has been in place for roughly four centuries, is responsible for much of what we regard as progress, and for much of what is destructive in our life, in our society, on the earth, and in our conscious-ness. For the sake of brevity, we can refer to it as the Cartesian/Newtonian view of reality, though other thinkers contributed to it. Some of its sources go back to the Greeks.

One prominent element in the framework is materialism. This is the assumption that the material world is the only true reality. Over the past few centuries, this view has become deeply rooted in the Western psyche, so much so that non-material realities have become deeply suspect and have been largely discarded. Our capacity to perceive non-material realities has atrophied. Today's cultural complex assumes that if something is not embodied in material form, it does not exist. Most of the scientific establish-ment will not touch it because it cannot be brought into the labo-ratory, tested empirically and proved or disproved. This myopic view of reality is reductionist, and it is untrue. The most crucial truths are so vast that they cannot be proved, though they can sometimes be experienced. This is the reason that science cur-rently has no definition for immaterial consciousness, other than an epiphenomenon, or byproduct, of brain functioning. The mental straitjacket of scientific skepticism is currently being chal-lenged by new knowledge thrown up by quantum physics, which deals with the nature of sub-atomic particles far beneath the level of possible perception. Physicists resort to mathematics to attempt to prove or disprove their ideas about this level of minute reality.

The early foundation of materialism was laid down by the atomistic theory of the ancient Greek, Democritus, around 400

B.C. He theorized that the basic building blocks of reality were tiny, indivisible particles of material, or atoms. By their collisions and combinations, all phenomena was created. Since the atom was conceived of as a tiny speck of material, and since it was the most basic reality, the atomistic theory created a bias toward materialism as the fundamental reality as it came down through two millennia of Western civilization to the present era.

Isaac Newton (1642-1727) elaborated on the atomistic theory and further developed materialism in the West. He established gravity as a universal force interacting between material objects, and announced three laws of motion—inertia, force, and equal reaction—that governed and explained the interactions of material objects with each other. In doing so, he laid the foundation for modern physics, the basis of the contemporary scientific worldview. It is probable that Newton himself believed in a deity, but his ideas fostered a cultural complex that discarded all non-manifest reality.

Rene Descartes (1596-1650) added another cornerstone to the modern Western worldview. He viewed the universe as an intricate, impersonal machine strictly ordered by mathematical laws—a material construction functioning like a clock. In addition, Descartes split off mind from matter in his inquiries, in effect ending the Western concern with non-material consciousness and focusing it exclusively on material questions.

The Cartesian/Newtonian cosmology established the foundation for a new worldview which has been in place ever since. It is a set of understandings that made possible the leaps in scientific understanding and technology that have occurred over the past 400 years. In those respects, it served us well. However, its influence increased the culture's disposition toward considering true reality to be exclusively material. A world of material objects presumes space between those objects. It also presumes that the space within which the objects are located is empty until filled by them. So, we experience today an empty cosmos of dead space, with only a few objects in it that are living. The space itself is immaterial, so it cannot have reality or life in it. A dead, empty cosmos is not a cosmos fit to live in. This worldview, unexamined and held largely in the unconscious, is responsible for the endemic loneliness, desolation and existential despair that we see in our civilization. We have lost our ground. We no longer feel that we belong to the cosmos. We no longer feel held by our universe. We are alienated and cut off from the life-force and from the source of sacredness. We pass this condition of suffering on to our children generation after generation, infecting them with the same meaninglessness, alienation and desolation that we have experienced in our own lives.

It turns out, however, that space is not empty. It is teeming with life and activity and Being. Quantum physicists have discovered that subatomic particles are emerging into existence in every cubic foot of space. They call this quantum foam. The particles are not arising from something else that is material. They are arising from nothingness, from the implicate order, from unmanifest potentiality. They appear from nowhere and quickly subside back into nothingness, back into space. This discovery quashes once and for all the notion of dead, empty space. It means that the entire universe is seething with livingness. The appearance and disappearance of the particles signals that they are crossing the line from Being in its unmanifest form, as living potentiality, to Being in its material form, or particles. We are seeing here how Being, itself invisible, becomes the world of visible forms. When the particles aggregate, they eventually become the apparently solid forms of our everyday life. Being is alive and in motion throughout the cosmos, including its space.

The Cartesian/Newtonian framework is an inadequate and dying worldview. Parts of it may be retained, but the basic idea of a non-living, exclusively material universe operating mechanically like a clock and filled with separate objects and empty space has outlived its useful life. It has become destructive of our society, our humanity, and our stewardship of the earth. It is reductionist and retrograde, an anachronism that threatens our very existence.

With luck, it is now disintegrating, as renewal gathers strength and waits in the wings.

4

The Field of Being

In a black void
of silent stillness,
Potential waited
in expectancy.
Feeling its Presence,
feeling its powers,
It filled with longing
To know itself and express itself.
Suddenly and magnificently,
Potential willed itself
into Creativity,
and hurled itself
in every direction.
It burst forth light,
it burst forth awareness,
it burst forth livingness,
it burst forth intelligence,
and made, of itself,
something from nothing—
a living Cosmos.

The Field of Being is ancient intuitive knowledge that has been lost in the Western world during the last 400 years. It is now being retrieved at an astonishing rate. Being is pure livingness. It is unmanifest. It is the ground of existence. It is pure potential prior to form. Physicist David Bohm called this unmanifest realm of pure potential the "implicate order," as opposed to the "explicate order," or the material realm. The Field of Being is beneath and generates everything that we see around us, but itself cannot be seen. It is alive, it is aware, it is conscious, and it is intelligent. Indeed, it is the principle of life, it is the principle of awareness, it is the principle of consciousness, and it is the principle of intelligence. It exists everywhere in the cosmic Field. It is the cosmos itself, conscious and alive.

The Field of Being is as vast as the cosmos. In recent years, a discipline called "field theory" emerged in the West. Its articulation has enabled us to more easily conceive of the Field of Being. Field theory originated in a study of electro-magnetic fields, after it was noted that molecules and particles behave in special ways within a field created by electricity and magnets, very differently from their behavior outside the field.

Field theory played an important part in the development of quantum physics. Inside a field, conditions are everywhere the same, making the interactions between molecules and particles similar in every part of the field. In other words, the field creates a special arena of reality, the influences of which are unique and constant and can be observed and understood.

Consideration of the cosmos as a single living field of intelligent consciousness is closer to science-fiction than to traditional religion. The conditions and operation of the Field are mysterious, even mind-boggling. First, the Field of the Cosmos is a Field of unity. It and everything in it are only one thing—Being. This truth was expressed in Hinduism's Vedanta 3,500 years ago:

> *"He is fire and the sun; he is the moon and stars, the air and the sea. He is this boy and that girl. He appears in countless different forms. He is the beginning, and he is the end. He is the source of all things. Each type of living being is distinct and different. But when we pierce the veil of difference, we see the unity of all beings."*

> *Svetasvatara Upanishad*

The truth of unity has been central to almost every spiritual discipline, excepting Christianity, ever since. It is central presently to quantum physics, one of whose basic ideas is the unified field. The most startling proof of the unified field in quantum physics was the discovery of non-locality. Since Newton promulgated his laws four hundred years ago, it has been bedrock science that causation must be local. In other words, a material object can only be affected by another material object colliding with it and transferring energy to it, in the manner of billiard balls. This is aside from gravity, which Newton also dealt with. Last century scientists, including a reluctant Einstein, discovered nonlocal causation. Two subatomic particles, after being associated with each other, were separated by some distance and then examined. Scientists were astounded to find that as they ascertained the spin of one particle, the spin of the other was determined, even though there was nothing between them to connect them. The realization was that the two particles were intimately connected by forces that were invisible, nonphysical and non-material. More accurately, at a deeper level the two particles were somehow one thing, a singularity. This shook the foundations of traditional, Newtonian science. It meant that our dominant, scientific explanation of reality was inaccurate and inadequate to explain reality. Forces unaccounted for were holding the universe together. It showed that reality is much more a web fundamentally linked together than a realm of objects standing separately in space, and affecting each other through collision.

Potentially, this discovery laid the foundation for dethroning the Newtonian understanding of the universe that we had accepted as truth for the past 400 years. It gave new and more profound meaning to the phrase "unified field."

Unable to include Being in their conceptual world, scientists asserted that this mysterious connection was the result of "the strong force" and "the weak interaction." These phrases are empty labels laid over connecting forces that the scientists are unable to explain. The assertion is basically that "something" is holding the world together. End of report. Might that "something" be living, intelligent, sentient Being? The scientists cannot go there because they are still trapped in the notion of a material, non-living cosmos. Many others of us, however, looking at the evidence, have no such trouble asserting that beneath the material world and binding it into a unity lies an implicate realm of conscious, living and intelligent Being. The drift of the modern world is inexorably in this direction. This is the direction of our evolution. We and the entire cosmos are one, living thing. Today, the convergence of these ancient and freshly minted realities is the most exciting development of our lifetime.

5

Levels of Being

Beyond silence,
wrapped in blackness,
the Absolute waits
in immensity.
Approaching its inner domain,
thoughts fail,
consciousness stills,
and wonder blooms
in black radiance.

Reality is layered. Each layer has its own laws and modes of operation. We are familiar with layered reality because we know and accept that, though at the level of our senses we live in a world of solid objects, at a microcosmic level those solid objects are composed of space, whirling atoms and subatomic particles. The world that we live in is unrecognizable at the levels revealed by the electron microscope. It is mostly space, living space.

Actually, the division of reality into layers or levels is artificial. Being itself is seamless and unitary, with no divisions, boundaries or sub-categories. From the standpoint of human understanding, however, it is practical to talk in terms of levels of Being.

The deepest, most mysterious and most inaccessible level of Being is the Absolute, the Ultimate Source. It is almost beyond our human capacity to perceive it. As we approach the Absolute our consciousness disappears into unconsciousness. Serious practitioners of meditation know this place well. It is a trance place of total blackness, total blankness, no experience, no perception, no thought. It is, in fact, unconsciousness generated by the Presence of Majesty. Coming closer to the Absolute, the mind is obliterated in its Presence. Perhaps the best way to have a glimpse of the

Absolute is somatically. Its Presence can be felt with the cells of the body—before awareness is totally extinguished. By definition, it is indescribable, majestic and infinitely mysterious.

Between the Absolute and the material realm, where we live and have our experience, are several intermediate stages of reality. These realms are more available to us. In fact, they are part of our common experience. The pure potentiality of the Absolute first generates a realm of vibration and energy. Next, it generates a realm of radiance and light. Next, it moves through a realm of pure imagery called the Mithal. Phenomena from these realms is woven into our physical and mental experience so integrally that it seems odd to consider them separately. Moving through these various levels and becoming progressively more dense, the Unmanifest becomes the Manifest.

The Absolute is the finest, most gossamer and most remote of the levels of reality. The material world, at the other end of the hierarchy or process, is the densest and heaviest realm. The material realm is the dying end of idea.

On its way to becoming material reality, material form becomes vibration, then light, then image, and finally material. This means that beneath the forms of the physical realm is a universe of pure radiance, shaping and holding the forms that emerge into materiality. Sometimes this realm of light can be seen fleetingly in the mind's eye, underlying and tracing the contours of the physical world. It comes through in the sparkle of sunlight on a lake.

The Mithal realm of pure imagery is accessible to our everyday experience. It is woven into the warp and weft of our consciousness and mental functioning. The mind-stream that we all experience daily is a stream of images, one after the other, linked in succession like pearls on a string. We perceive and make sense of reality, make our decisions and live our lives on the basis of our experiences with this stream of imagery. In our inner experience, the images are woven together with language. In the sequence of evolution, however, the two were separate. The capacity for imagery developed millennia before language.

Every invention of the human species, before appearing at the material level, first passes through this level of imagery. A bicycle, for example, was not possible until the image of a workable bicycle organized itself in consciousness. Einstein's discoveries of the relativity of time and space took place in the Mithal, as he envisioned himself riding on one of two trains speeding through space. The discovery of the molecular structure of benzene by Friedrich Kekule also took place in the Mithal, in a dream of a snake eating its tail. When he awoke, he realized that the image encapsulated the answer to the scientific question that he had been posing.

The Mithal is also the realm where archetypes reside. Carl Jung's work made us aware of the immense importance of the play of archetypal images. Held at the unconscious level, these deep, culturally shared images influence every aspect of human life.

6

The Unfolding

On the third day of Spring,
life yearns for itself.
Winter's apple tree,
touched by the sun,
and nourished by the dew,
waits high on a hill,
bare and expectant.
Then life gathers,
life surges,
from the core of the earth
through the roots of the tree
to the tips of the limbs,
to the welcoming buds.
Breaking open
by silent signal,
the buds flow out their exuberance.
White radiance.
This moment has been in preparation
for a billion years.
They bloom forth,
first one,
then another,
then hundreds and thousands.
The tree, clothed over
with fresh and lovely life,
now sits, resplendent, sublime,
life blooming its artless perfection
into a breathless and waiting world.

The universe is profoundly, primordially creative. It is the principle of creativity itself. The unfolding of the Cosmos from the fireball to the present, over 13.7 billion years, is one single extended creative event. The creations of the cosmos are creative, as it flows through them and sustains them in existence. The creativity has been unfolding itself for billions of years, bringing into existence and metamorphosing the cosmos. This unfolding has a number of unique and observable characteristics.

First, there is no planning, no considering, no weighing of alternatives. Being does not function like a human being. It simply manifests. The material realm emerges in an endless, seamless process over unimaginable stretches of time. The project is never finished. There is no fade-out. The resources are infinite and changes along the way are inexorable and startling. Looking backward, we can observe the pattern of the unfolding. It is not possible to anticipate its future, though if we are fully awake, the unfolding of the present moment can be perceived with wonder.

Looking back at the development of life on earth, we can see milestones in the creation of life. In a watery environment of non-life, living cells appeared. They learned how to access and metabolize energy and sustain themselves. One cell moved inside another cell, providing a nucleus and making possible a memory bank of DNA. The newly nucleated cell learned to replicate itself, complete with nucleus, which eventually culminated in colonies of cells that became coherent organisms. We each exist today as a colony not unlike a coral reef, an aggregation of independent, living cellular entities, each co-operating and doing its specific job to keep the colony, our organic entity, thriving.

In the developing lifeforms in the ocean, the universe invented the nervous system, eyes, hearts and the circulatory system, digestion and excretion, sexual organs for reproduction and other wondrous necessities for life. Each development was an astounding manifestation of primordial creativity, a steady unfolding of possibilities, a metamorphosis of existing realities into something new and startling. Life moved out of the oceans onto the land, first with plants and then with fish that eventually became animals. The story is familiar, but our sense of wonder at it has somewhat eroded. A world of reptiles developed, of all sizes, configurations and habits, and then that creation was destroyed. This opened the way for a world of mammals, which articulated itself into the diversity of species that we know today.

One of those mammals, a primate in the trees, came down onto the savannahs, stood upright on two legs, began to make tools and developed language and social co-operation. Eventually that primate's consciousness expanded from simple animal consciousness of its surroundings and internal states into self-consciousness. It became aware of its own awareness. It discovered the possibilities of agriculture, culture and society. The human being emerged and thrived. Altogether, the story of the unfolding is a study in glorious, jaw-dropping creativity, from the unicellular to the human.

The second aspect of the universe's creativity that is apparent in surveying these developments is unceasing transformation. Over and over, existing realities transmute into totally new and different life-forms. Fish become animals. Animals become humans. If the new life-forms are successful in accessing energy supplies, usually by consuming other life-forms, and in reproducing themselves with offspring, they find a place in the shifting tapestry of life. If not, they disappear, and their place is taken by more successful life-forms. It is estimated that 99% of all life-forms that have ever existed on Earth have disappeared. All forms, over vast expanses of time, are metamorphosing into new forms. Darwin, of course, called this evolution.

This metamorphosis has the quality of self-transcendence. Building on existing realities, it develops ever greater complexity and pushes organisms into ever new possibilities. Increasing complexification is one of the hallmarks of Being's creativity.

A third characteristic of the cosmos is infinite organizing power. In metamorphosing itself, the universe can do an infinite number of things all at the same time and correlate them all with each other. In a deep interrelationship of all parts that is apparent in any eco-system, everything fits perfectly into the whole and everything fits with all the other parts. Parts that do not fit disappear. Each piece of reality nourishes, enhances and supports the others and each contributes its piece to the whole system. This is integration at the fundamental level of Being.

Language fails in the face of the infinite creativity of Being. The systems and organisms that Being manifests are themselves permeated with its creativity. We are aware of creativity in ourselves, and generally we assume that individual human beings are the source of that capacity for innovation. On the contrary, the Field is the source of all creativity. The impulses that prompt humans to create cultural artifacts are pure Being. The objects that emerge from the hands and brains of humans as a result of the impulses are pure Being. Being's own deepest nature is to express itself. We are the means or the conduits of that expression. It is a great experience and a privilege to participate in the creative process of Being. It is one of the most exciting and fulfilling and mysterious things that a human can do. Every creative artist knows the deep thrill when the power of Being's creativity wells up in the body and mind to bring forth something new. A flow of energy is experienced in the body. Synthesis and innovation arrive. There is an impression of being unerringly guided in a spillover of emergence as everything comes together in coherence. Something new emerges that never existed before. This process could better be called co-creation. The human provides the fingers and the brain, but Being provides the deep impulse and the motive push.

7

The Holding

A quiet time,
in silence.
I turn my cells outward,
searching.
Then it is there,
a dynamic, living Presence,
mysterious, veiled, elusive,
but strongly present.
I am suddenly held.
My spirits lift.
My vision expands,
and I am irrigated
by the gifts of its nature
as they flow through me—
joy, strength, peace
and uncounted other sensations
of well-being.
Suffused in gratitude,
I burst into flower.

Whether or not we notice, we are being held by Being. We are embedded in a matrix of livingness that sustains our existence during every moment of our lives. "The Holding" is a fundamental archetype in humans. It is associated with our earliest interactions with our mother, the physical and emotional tone and impact of being touched and cradled by her, and also with the entire environment of safety, security and loving nurture around the child. It carries emotional experiences of bonding and protection. A good holding environment can produce a self-confident, secure adult with a great deal of basic trust. An inadequate or seriously defective holding can create life-long emotional problems of insecurity, vulnerability, fear and lack of trust.

The baby arrives at birth still somewhat unformed. Structures in its psyche are still in the process of gelling. The experiences of the holding environment, good or bad, are the templates around which that final stage of formation takes place. A great deal of fine work has been done in the past few decades to track the unfolding development of the child's psyche. It usually goes under the name of child development or object relations theory. These clumsy labels refer to the formative impact of the interactions of the child, the subject, with its first object, the mother. From these first seminal interactions, mental structures are formed and relations to all other and later objects in the world are influenced. Developmental psychologists have articulated the needs of the child for support and mirroring at each stage of its development, and the resulting problems if the child does not receive what it needs from the environment. As adults we live through the mental structures formed around the early holding experiences. A lens is created through which we interact with the world for the rest of our lives. Our worldview, our perceptions of reality, and our experiences as adults are all filtered through the early experiences of the holding. Although we continue to be shaped by our experiences throughout life, this extreme sensitivity to the environment lasts, it is estimated, from birth to about four years old. In a very real way, the holding that we were given determines who we become. Our psyche, with all it idiosyncratic quirks, is a direct result of the holding environment that we received.

Unfortunately, in our culture very few people receive a truly healthy holding during the formative period. No mother can always have food ready when hunger strikes the baby. Diapers cannot always be changed instantly. The baby begins very early to experience gaps in its holding, experiences of discomfort and pain that register on its psyche as shocks not understood. Each incident of discomfort acts as a small rent in its holding. Each of the negative experiences crystallizes and goes into the psyche, to eventually be incorporated into the expectations in the adult worldview, coloring and influencing all our later experiences in the world.

As life progresses, the need for holding does not diminish. It remains an important component at all stages. Loss of the holding environment is a major issue for young people leaving the family and going out into the world on their own. Negotiating this passage can be a major source of anxiety, vulnerability and even trauma, as they struggle to find their feet outside the accustomed holding of the family.

When it comes time to form our own family, the holding is again a prominent issue in the development. All long-lasting and important relationships are, in a sense, based on the unspoken contract: " I will hold you in your pain, fear and vulnerability if you will hold me in my pain, fear and vulnerability." We speak unceasingly of love as the basis for relationship, and it is important, but the state of love does not sustain itself and usually evolves itself into something more mundane. The unspoken core understanding around mutual holding is much more basic and central. It is actually the glue that holds the relationship together over time.

The most important holding of all is the holding by Being. The world is a harsh, dangerous and sometimes infinitely cruel place. We know this, and yet we must make our way through it and live our lives. As our perception of unmanifest, living Being has atrophied over the past few centuries in the West, we have become more isolated, more alienated, more threatened, more desolate, and more neurotic. We have lost the holding of Being. We have lost our belonging. We have progressed from the experiences of primitive peoples of being held and immersed in an ocean of Life and Being to feeling separate, alone and threatened. We are alienated from the very ground of our Being. Without the experience of the holding of Being, we feel empty, and we turn to the world and claw at it to try to get the security, safety and the other gifts of that holding. It rarely works, and if so, not for long. The unstable, shifting world cannot reliably supply these gifts. They can only come, in the last analysis, from Being. We look in all the wrong places for what we need, and, fearful and in despair, overlook what is always present to solve the problem.

The holding of Being is always there. Our solution is to become aware of it. We are in a state of self-induced amnesia about the holding of Being. We need to wake up and widen the screen of our awareness. It is apparent, once we turn toward it, that the holding of Being is present and unlimited. The sun arrives each morning with its gifts of light and warmth. The earth, fecund and fertile, offers us food and water. The gases in the air, with 21% oxygen, are perfectly balanced for us to breathe. Our hearts, our lungs, our kidneys, and all of our other organs are all doing their job faithfully, outside of our direction or instruction. The cells of our body are similarly co-operating in a trillion interactions per second to keep our organism functioning. Again, totally outside our direction. We have friends, and perhaps family, to share our triumphs and failures. We have galaxies whirling around us in perfect order and balance. All of the eco-systems of the earth, on which our survival depends, interact to keep themselves functioning despite our mistakes. At a macro level, all is in order. This all adds up to a vast holding that is provided every moment for us, and is difficult to overlook.

All of this support and holding by Being generally goes unnoticed and unappreciated, as we focus on our problems, our fears, and our needs of the moment. With only a little reorientation, however, a little turning toward it, we can become aware that we are being held by Being, supported and nurtured in every moment.

It is a wondrous thing to be born a human, with the gift of this miraculous consciousness. It is a wondrous thing to be offered the potential of unfolding our gifts into the world. It is a wondrous thing to be held by Being and to experience the miraculous universe as we metamorphose our way through life. Our response should perhaps include a sense of wonder, a sense of mystery, a sense of awe, and a swelling of gratitude for the gifts ceaselessly bestowed on us by Being.

8

The Conscious Universe

Naked came I,
but not alone,
into this realm
of changing forms,
to stretch and reach
for nameless touch,
to merge and grow,
and lose myself
when Presence comes,
to know I'm held
by mystery,
to reach into the
depths of life,
For this I came.

The most fundamental reality of the universe is consciousness, not material. The basic assumption of our culture about reality has been wrong for almost 400 years. Our assumption that material is the basic reality in the cosmos is mistaken. On the contrary, the universe is pure mind, pure consciousness, pure awareness. The material realm is a by-product of the ocean of consciousness, only an effect of its cause.

Quantum scientists talk today of the universe existing in "quantum soup." This concept is very close to the concept of a conscious universe. Add livingness and awareness and that "quantum soup" becomes Being, the matrix out of which the material world mysteriously emerges.

There is nothing remote or unfamiliar about consciousness. Each of us has access to it constantly. The awareness that we each experience in our mind is the same consciousness of which the universe is composed. At any moment, we can turn our attention to regard the pool of pure awareness that our images, concepts and thoughts move through. When we do this, we will observe a field of extraordinary sensitivity, with the capacity to create, record, receive and hold images and thoughts. This is a field of impressionability. The world, inner and outer, presses itself into a waiting receptive field of impressionability. The pool of awareness is fundamentally who we are. The body is secondary, an attachment to the pool. The awareness is what the universe is. The material world is secondary to it. The ocean of awareness is Being itself. Being and the field of consciousness are fundamentally the same thing. Living consciousness is the most basic characteristic of Being. Being is living consciousness, unmanifest, awake, aware and creative.

Science is currently bound up with study of the brain as the source of consciousness. It has no definition of consciousness other than as an epiphenomenon, or by-product, of brain functioning. In these pursuits, the areas of the brain have been extensively mapped, and connected to states and mental experiences. Severely limited by the assumptions of materialism, which crowds them into the necessary conclusion that the material brain is somehow producing immaterial consciousness, scientists are unable to explain this great leap from one realm to another.

Some scientists are beginning to investigate the possibility that the brain is not producing consciousness but rather filtering it into the human system. For healthy functioning to be uninterrupted, the brain would have to be undamaged, whether it is the source of consciousness or merely its filter. We are edging toward the realization that the brain functions like a transducer. A transducer converts one type of energy into another. For instance, a telephone is acting as a transducer when it converts electrical signals into vibrations or words that we can understand in the receiver. The brain is a transducer when it converts pure awareness streaming into it into human thoughts, images and concepts that we experience.

Further, the view that consciousness is produced by the brain does not sync with the emerging realization of the singularity of the unified field. In a unified field, instances of paranormal communication, where one person picks up content in the consciousness of another, are not anomalies but to be expected. Sharing a field of consciousness obviously allows experiences of shared content, which are not explicable in the current scientific model. In spite of the growing number of young scientists who are studying paranormal phenomena, and the growing base of reliable data that shows the phenomena to be real, mainstream science continues to reject both the paranormal communication and the thesis that consciousness originates in the field outside the brain. This is in spite of the agreement on the unified field, and the axiom that nothing in a field can contain qualities or characteristics that are not inherent in the field itself. Having recognized the existence of the unified field, now an incontrovertible part of quantum physics, perhaps the incorporation of consciousness into the field is in the offing at some not too future date.

9

Living Light

I am here.
I am here, shining and incandescent.
I am here in a million, million patterns
of light, of symmetry and of beauty.
I am the patterns of light that shine forth
from under the covering of the material world.
I am the radiant patterns of light
in nature, in mathematics, in language,
in art, in architecture, and in all created forms.
I am the eternal, self-luminous Earth of Light,
shining forth
in countless, intricate, beautiful patterns
all around you.
I am the web of light and life
that holds all living things together.
I am always here,
beneath the material world
and sustaining the material world.
You can always reach me,
and touch me, and see me.
I am the living patterns that shine.
The whole of Earth
and all of its forms
are shining with one brilliant radiance.

Radiance is a fundamental characteristic of the universe. Radiance is embodied in the sun, that marvelous, life-giving presence in our sky every day. The earth and the Sun are locked in a harmonious embrace, a wonderful dance of creation. Everything that exists as life on the earth is here because the sun comes up predictably every day and showers itself upon us. It is much more than light and warmth. It is living light.

It passes living light and life itself to all the organisms of the earth. In doing so, it incrementally sacrifices itself for the life that it makes possible. The sun burns by transforming hydrogen into helium at fantastic, explosive temperatures. In producing its heat and light, it burns up 4 million tons of itself every second. This is not a big worry because it is approximately one million times as big as the Earth. The sun is continually giving itself away to make life possible on earth. In time, perhaps five billion years, a little longer than the earth has existed, it will exhaust itself and become a dark and burned out shell. In the meantime, we are the recipients of its fabulous gifts.

The gifts of the sun are able to be received by a grateful Earth because of a remarkable invention 3 billion years ago. In the earliest stages of life on Earth, a molecule figured out how to capture sunlight and use it as food for energy. This chlorophyll molecule learned to receive photons of light, which are small chariots of energy, as they stream from the sun and into the earth. It learned to capture the photons, store them, and transform them into energy for its life processes. Every successful organism has to solve the problem of finding an energy source to feed on and sustain itself. The solution achieved by the chlorophyll molecule was brilliant but unlikely. Streaming sunlight is always available, but capturing its photons and transforming them into food is a big achievement, to say the least. And, all of this without arms or eyes or brain. We call the process that it invented photosynthesis. Once it had solved the sunlight/energy equation, the pathway opened for brilliant success and expansion on Earth. Plants developed in the ocean, came out onto the land and blanketed the earth.

Other organisms in the ocean found different solution to the energy problem. Primarily, they began to obtain energy by eating each other. This was also a successful strategy, and marine life developed apace, came out onto the land, and became the animals. Even the animals who fed on each other, however, were dependent on the gifts of sunlight and photosynthesis, because the energy was passed through the food chain to them--from the sun to the photosynthesizing plants, to the animals who ate the plants, and finally to the animals who ate the animals who ate the plants. At the base of the whole developing system remains the bursting energy of the sun showering life on Earth.

Radiance is also part of our life in ways other than sunlight. The wisdom traditions for thousands of years have intuitively detected a realm of light lying beneath the covering of the material world. More gossamer, less dense and self-illumined, this layer of living light is life itself, Being itself, in the process of becoming material. This level of living light is subtle, and generally available to our perception only in the mind's eye. Occasionally, however, it leaks over into the material realm and shows itself. It is old news now that auras, living light emitted from humans, other animals and even plants, can be registered on photographic film. As we know, some people are sensitized enough to see auras in their daily lives. Perhaps one day we will all have this ability. We appear to be evolving in that direction.

Living light emitted from the interior of humans has also been captured and measured recently in scientific experiments. The German scientist Fritz Popp has successfully constructed a machine that registers very low amounts of light protons as they emerge from the human body. He has proved that there is a tiny current of light coming out of living systems.

Popp speculates that the source of the light in a living system may be the DNA, and that its purpose may be to constantly beam instructions to the organism's cells to keep the system in trim. Further, the light may serve as communications between organisms, a kind of bio-emission that weaves life-forms together. Plants that depend on each other's processes may be sending signals carried by light, regarding their mutual organic needs of the moment. Similar signals may be carried between plants and insects, for example, between flowers and bees, which survive interdependently.

We are in the early stages of discovering that life is vastly more complex, more layered and operating on more non-material levels than our materialistic science has suspected. The great adventure still lies ahead.

10

The Web of Being

As I rested on the mountain peak,
a great cloud of fog
rose up and enfolded me.
Whiteness reigned.
Then, as I watched,
the fog made itself into shapes.
Wonderful shapes.
Infinitely varied and miraculous
and lovely shapes.
The fog disappeared
and I saw that the wonderful shapes
were the shapes of the world
that I live in.

The space of the Cosmos is filled with teeming life, movement, energy, and information. In every cubic foot of space, countless sub-atomic particles are appearing from space and almost instantaneously disappearing back into space. Quantum physics tells us that they are coming into manifest form from their nature as unmanifest waveforms. After a brief residence in the world of forms, they disappear back into their waveforms. In effect, these particles are constantly crossing the boundary from spirit, or the implicate order, to matter, the explicate order. This is happening everywhere in the cosmos.

The waveforms are in contact with each other throughout the universe. They are passing information from one to another rippling outward in expanding circles to the far reaches of the Cosmos. And, this happens instantaneously. The process is not limited to the speed of light. So, the Cosmos instantly records everything that occurs in it. The entire field gets the information. We are beginning to understand that space in the Cosmos is a vast information system. Physicists Carl Pribram and Walter Schemp theorized that the contents of our mind, and even our memories, are stored not in the brain but in the web of information in space. We simply access it when we need it.

Through the interaction of this giant web of waveforms, everything is linked. We ourselves are exchanging particles with the space around us. We are exchanging particles with the people and things around us. We are interpenetrating the universe. It is our deepest nature. We are woven into this warp and weft of the universe in the most fundamental way, physically as well as consciously. The web of waveforms is a physical analog for Being itself. It is the ground of the world, the matrix out of which manifestation springs. We are not just related to everything. In a very real sense, we are everything. At the deepest level, there is just one thing in the universe, the Field, pure Being, generative and evolving. We are an integral component of that one thing.

In the current epoch, we are evolving past the archetype of God as a king, at the top of a hierarchy of life, ruling, creating, dispensing justice, punishing, and rewarding. This archetype of God has been in place in our collective psyche for more than five thousand years. It is a phase of our development which we have outgrown and which is now coming to an end.

A new archetype of God is forming as we watch. It is entirely different from the archetype of God as king, a large human. It is an image of a field of pure potential and pure creativity. The archetypal image is of a body or cloud of radiant, generative, living fog. It is more impersonal than the king archetype, but has fabulous capabilities. The radiant fog is alive, conscious, and given to shape-shifting. It can be seen as a fog of subatomic wave/particles aggregating themselves into forms, each particle playing its unique part to create the temporary, metamorphosing material world. For a period, the particles dedicate themselves to sustaining the three-dimensional form. In due time, they separate and the form disappears. Viewed dispassionately from this perspective, our world, the forms and beings in it, and the material universe itself have the quality of a three-dimensional hologram changing slowly over millennia. Reality is not real in the solid way that it appears to us to be real. In a certain sense, it has a virtual character. A mountain is only a temporary arrangement of particles rather than the mountain that we have always perceived. Our own bodies are similar. Nothing endures except the Field itself. Absolutely everything inside the Field eventually disappears back into it.

Our job, as components in this sound and light show, is to keep the Field and its wondrous properties and processes forefront in our consciousness. We must endeavor to understand reality truly as it is happening, and appreciate the gift of participating in it.

11

Democratic Divinity

I am Value itself,
come to fruition
in a thousand different forms.
Hear me, feel me, know me,
but you can't see me.
I am too subtle for you,
with your demands for
separateness and significance.
I am too high for you,
with your endless quest for meaning.
I am too deep for you,
in your confusion and superficiality.
But I am always here,
pushing you toward me,
toward more development,
more awareness, and
more contact with me.
I am the impulse toward
more life.

In a living, cosmic field of Being, or sub-atomic particles, every particle is equally divine. This is the nature of a field. Conditions within a field, in this case the universe, are uniform throughout the field. In science, these conditions would go under the name of "natural law." The prime mover in science over the past 400 years has been the quest to discover natural law, the way the universe functions. The latest discoveries in this respect reveal the universe to be a Field, a unified Field. It is only in our lifetime that we have moved into position to consider the universe as one vast, unified Field.

Considering each particle in the Field to be equally alive, equally intelligent, equally generative and equally divine makes the leap from secular to sacred. Each particle, like every other particle, is Being itself. Altogether they form the Field, which is Being and which is divine. From the depths of itself, the Field produces three-dimensional forms, which are arrangements composed of divine particles and so are themselves divine. The particles aggregate to form our world and our universe, the entirety of which is divine. Nothing exists, or ever could exist, outside of this divine ocean. After centuries of being split into polarized camps, science and spirituality are converging at last into this fundamental understanding. Evolution is moving us apace.

The importance of moving from the archetype of God as King to God as Field is almost incalculable. Archetypes held in the unconscious shape our perception of human life and reality. The King archetype rests on the concept of hierarchy as the basic model underlying all life. The vertical arrangement of hierarchy allows and endorses the perception that beings at the top of the hierarchical ladder are supremely important, beings just below the top are very important, and beings near the bottom are not important at all. In other words, hierarchy validates the operation of status. Through the millennia, hierarchy, held unconsciously as the primary archetype in the collective psyche, has validated all manner of distortions in human life. Holding the hierarchical archetype makes possible the justification of racism, as well as gender discrimination and all other forms of domination and oppression. It is the antithesis of equality.

The concept of hierarchy is very close to the concept of polarity. Each pulls reality apart into split camps. Hierarchy pulls it apart in a vertical manner, separating high from low, and generally assigning value to the high. Polarity splits reality in a horizontal way, creating opposites—good/bad, beautiful/ugly, valuable/

valueless, secular/spiritual, etc.—and assigning value to one pole or the other. Both hierarchy and polarity violate the fundamental principle of the singularity of the unified field, as the wisdom traditions have pointed out for many centuries. Getting beyond these splits could transform our individual and collective consciousness.

The Field archetype offers a corrective. Considering every particle in the Field to be equally divine changes the lens entirely. Every single thing composed of particles would have equal value and sacredness, whether living or inanimate. Discrimination and rejection are not consonant with the Field as the fundamental basis of reality. The democratic divinity of particles, that is to say, their identity and equality as minute, divine components of the field, would confer divinity upon all of creation. If we could live from the unconsciously held assumption of a miraculous, living and creative Field composed of miraculous, living and creative particles, all of which are equally important and equally divine, it might help us learn not to trash our world. Value would be conferred by simple existence in the Field. Distinctions that we now make between the valuable and the worthless would be groundless. Life would look very different from this perspective.

We might be able to find our way back to a sense of the sacredness of the earth and life itself. We might be able to view the universe with a sense of wonder. We might be able to re-enchant our existence by fully realizing the miraculous nature of life in the living Field around us.

12

The Unfolding

I will hold the space
for you to unfold your gifts.
I will make a place
for new possibilities to appear.
Resting deep and silent,
I will tolerate chaos,
and turn it into order.
I will create beauty
and intensify it into suffering.
All things are crucial,
And nothing truly matters.
I am at play.

From its explosive beginning 13.7 billion years ago, the universe has slowly and dynamically unfolded itself. It has its own unique style of doing so. It takes its time, eons if necessary, and unfolds new developments and creations so that they fit perfectly and completely into the existing framework previously created. There may be some trial and error involved in this process, but the incorporation of the new, when finished, is perfection itself. The old and the new are infinitely collated together. Order emerges out of chaos. Perfect balance is achieved as all parts, old and new, are correlated with each other. The results are self-transcending. The process continues, inexorably and eternally, to create a breathtaking work of resolved art.

The story of the universe is the story of this unfolding drama. It has chapters of violence and cataclysm, but after a run of 13.7

billion years, has worked things out pretty well, as we can see when we look around our world.

The first chapter in the story, after the spectacular burst of the beginning, was the creation of galaxies. The gases and particles blown outward by the Big Bang first traveled at too great a velocity to form material forms. Over time, however, as they traveled into expanding space, they slowed to just the speed necessary to form aggregations of matter. The conditions had to be perfect. A faster velocity would not have allowed the gases and particles to coalesce into matter. A slower velocity would likewise have not allowed their formation. In these necessarily perfect conditions, billions of galaxies formed. The expansion has now slowed, so that the ideal conditions no longer exist. There will be no new galaxies. We will have to make do with the billion, billion galaxies that came out of this transient, perfectly balanced set of conditions.

The next step in the unfolding was the creation of stars. Gravity collapsed the gases and particles of matter in the galaxies into coherent entities that caught fire. Converting hydrogen atoms into helium atoms, perfect conditions allowed the developing stars to shower their light and warmth out into the black deep. Planets coalesced and took up regular orbits around the stars. Bits of extraneous matter became moons, and they took up orbits around the planets. The system was now ready and waiting for life. The stage was set. The next stage of the unfolding could begin.

Our sun was, of course one of those stars, As the planets in our solar system came together and fell into their orbits around the sun, only Earth was a fertile field for the next act of the drama. The Earth was exactly the right size to unfold life. Its gravitational forces, a function of its size, were strong enough to hold it together, and to form a crust on the surface while the center of the planet remained molten and mobile. Mars was too small. It became a dead rock, solid clear through to the center. Jupiter was too large. It could not pull its gases and material together with its gravity, and so remained almost entirely gaseous.

Around Earth, an atmosphere of gases formed, shielding the surface of the planet from the harsh intensity of the sun's rays. This allowed life to begin. On Earth, the rains began. It rained for a very, very long time, forming the oceans. This water was crucial to the next step in the unfolding, the development of life. Like sunlight, water is life. Living organisms are, in part, living water.

The gathered water provided a perfect environment for the creation of single-celled organisms, the first life. One cell moved invasively into another to form a nucleus, and that made possible multi-celled organisms made of nucleated cells. The nucleus of the cells functions like a storage bank of DNA, which provided a form of memory. Now the multi-celled organisms could reproduce themselves.

A great variety of marine life blossomed, and then life moved out of the oceans onto the land. There the unfolding continued apace. Life-forms metamorphosed over millennia, and today here we sit as the result. This story, this unfolding, is our story. It is our heritage and our personal history. The biography of each of us includes a phase as a galaxy, a star, a planet, a single cell, a multi-celled marine organism, an animal, and, now, a human line of antecedents. We are the universe itself, unfolded through eons and metamorphosing in shape and nature to what we are today. The process is not finished. The story is on-going. The miraculous unfolding continues eternally.

The latest act in the story is, like the other acts, surprising, unexpected, and even astounding. Having created a multiplicity of life-forms on a perfectly balanced planet in a solar system conducive to life, one of those life-forms, in a leap of evolution, developed self-awareness and then language. These remarkable events allowed that privileged life-form, ourselves, to observe and become aware of the story of the universe. This is precisely where we are today. We are now registering our history, our identity as the universe. The universe, through us, is revealing its story to itself, becoming aware of its own glory. Having exuberantly created and unfolded the drama, Being now turns back, through us, to look at its handiwork.

13

The Optimal Thrust

I am the Light
that sparkles on icicles.
I am the wind
that caresses the leaves.
I am the movement
of the slowly turning earth.
I am always here.
I am in no hurry.
I do things my way.

Looking back over the story of the universe, it is apparent that the unfolding did not occur in a random manner. The field does not operate in a mindless, mechanical mode. There is observable pattern and design in the unfolding. There is coherence. There is direction, and there is an arc to the story line. The universe is unfolding itself with a thrust toward the optimal. It is slowly moving itself toward more consciousness, more complexity, and more variety. It has a bias toward more life.

When we try to grasp this invisible force that is coordinating and giving coherence to the unfolding, we can scarcely conceive it. It consists of an intelligent dynamic in the unfolding. It is much more in the process itself, the collation and organization of the discrete steps in the process. There is no one thing in particular to see, no one thing to grab onto and say: "See! This is evidence of intelligence working!"

The case for living intelligence in the cosmos must rest finally on its handiwork as a whole, and on the story of how it got to this place where we find ourselves today.

It is estimated that there are one trillion interactions and pro-cesses occurring every second in order to keep a human body alive. We know with certainly that our bodies are composed of a vast number of cells, each of which is a separate, living entity. Under the proper conditions, each cell can live on its own outside the body. We are, in actuality, a composite creature, a colony of cells that, like a coral reef, builds a single, functioning whole. We are a walking, talking, thinking, fleshy composite of countless, seething, individual life-forms.

The current work in stem-cell research underlines this view. The same stem-cell, according to demands, can become an eye cell or a kidney cell or a brain cell. Its eventual function in the body does not depend on its own unchangeable nature, but rather on some mysterious quality of Being that endows it with the capaci-ties that are needed for the task at hand. It is being organized by the Field to meet the demands of life. Life is shaping the stem-cell to fulfill the functions momentarily required by life. This is the miraculous quality of the Field in full regalia, operating right in front of our eyes, the optimal thrust made visible.

Creatures on Earth are also in a mutually dependent dance with the first life-form on the planet—bacteria. In the primeval oceans, bacteria were the first to appear. They diversified exponen-tially, as they found different solutions to life's questions around survival. Some of them ate each other to exist. Others divided up the work and formed co-operative, mutually enhancing unions. They became symbiotic partners in the dance of the Field. It is estimated that there are more than 25,000 types of bacteria liv-ing on Earth. They are everywhere, including inside the human system. As resident co-journers, they perform a myriad of crucial, vital functions in our system. They help break down food and turn it into nutrients that can be used, they assist excretion, they assist in the bloodstream, and much more. The list is very long. As organisms, we act as host to these tiny life-forms. We provide them with conditions essential to their survival, and in return they perform vital life functions on which our own existence depends.

The organization, integration and sheer design value inherent in the cellular and bacterial functions in our body are startling. There is nothing mechanical about these interactions. They are fully organic, more like a flower than a clock. They are a marvel of design, interweaving the oldest life-forms, bacteria and cells, into the very core of current life-forms, ourselves. There is deep intelligence at work here, a formidable intelligence beyond our capacity to comprehend. The Field is at work here, expressing itself in livingness, intricacy, and complex systems that are wonderful to behold. We humans are the beneficiaries of these capabilities. We are both the results and the beneficiaries of the Field's slowly unfolding optimal thrust.

14

Consciousness

I am a pool
of living awareness,
of light, energy and
intelligence,
surrounded by a sea,
of living awareness,
of light, energy and
intelligence.
This sea and I are one.
Our qualities are one,
Our consciousness is one.
How could I have ever thought
that I was separate and alone?

The Field of the Cosmos is not only seething with living, sub-atomic particles, it is alive with consciousness. We are having to work our way back to the truth that consciousness is an omnipres-ent, ethereal presence in the universe. Descartes, 400 years ago, separated consciousness from the body and from matter. Effective inquiry into consciousness in the West was frozen at that point, as the world followed and built on Descartes' vision, including his mechanical view of the universe. It could have been different. Ancient cultures almost universally conceived the universe to be a vast, living and conscious arena, pervaded by a life-force that was the source of health and life. Generally, they anthropomorphized the life-force into an archetypal image of a God or a Goddess that embodied the force. Beneath the images, however, were percep-tions of livingness and consciousness abroad in the universe.

Perhaps there is treasure in the trash. Perhaps the West was fulfilling a deep need in human evolution by focusing on the material realm to the exclusion of all unmanifest realities. The intense concentration of the West on manifest reality, matter and its inter-actions, has unfolded the secrets and workings of matter extremely quickly and efficiently. It has moved our evolution along exponentially, and changed our lives and our possibilities beyond recognition. We are much the better for it.

However, at this point in time a correction is needed. The exclusive concentration of science on matter has left us alienated and desolate, an intruder in our own cosmic home. Without the experience of the living ocean of Being as the context of our experience, human life has become trivial and de-sacralized. Dropping spirit out of human life has dropped our heart out. It has left us disoriented and confused, lost in a dead, empty and threatening universe. It has abstracted the living core from life, leaving a dry, empty husk behind.

In this context, the present, on-going scientific inquiry into consciousness is investigating how, but not if, the brain produces consciousness. The mechanical model of Descartes simmers beneath the entire project. The research is yielding useful results, as the brain is mapped and specific areas are correlated with various human functions. However, a brain functioning as a filter would operate in the same manner. On the prime question of the source of consciousness, the research is reductive and blinkered. The basic question of the source of consciousness is evidently not being asked.

A few intrepid researchers are venturing out of the box to explore whether consciousness might reside outside the brain in the Field. Carl Pribram and Walter Schemp have seriously investigated the possibility that consciousness is both within and outside our bodies, that our brains do not generate consciousness but simply receive it from the Field. In this line of thought, even our memories may be stored outside us in the Field, and accessed through frequencies as needed. This view considers that our brain, like the Field around us, makes use of quantum processes. We know that the Field of quantum wave/particles is a Field of information. We know that energy and information are encoded and transferred through the Field of wave/particles. The new views of consciousness are bringing our speculations about the brain into line with what we know about the Field. The boundaries between ourselves and the Field are being progressively eroded. One day, perhaps, after further evolution, we will be able to perceive ourselves as one with the Field, not just joined together but rather a singularity. We are the Field. It is our basic nature, and the basic nature of the universe. And, it is the basic nature of all creation.

The new research on consciousness is just beginning to open doors for further inquiry into the possibilities. It is, of course, fiercely resisted by scientists of the old school, who continue locked into explanations based on the mechanistic model. It may take some time and considerable good research to move the scientific establishment off dead center. In the meantime, the rest of us are perfectly free to evolve at our own pace. We each have our own pool of consciousness to contemplate. We are free to move ourselves into a larger view, the view that we exist and are an integral part of a vast ocean of living, intelligent consciousness that is our own basic nature. If we choose, we can watch the play of the Field of consciousness as it unfolds itself over time, and expresses its basic nature and creativity in material and immaterial form.

The world of forms is emerging from the Field of consciousness. This is the same thing as saying that the world of forms is emerging from the Field of sub-atomic particles. There is no split between consciousness and particles. The particles are alive. Their nature is consciousness. We can scarcely get our minds around the miracle of living consciousness. It is at the heart of all creation, the core of the universal Field. Before our eyes, science is in the process of proving the miraculous.

15

Balance

Grow larger and larger,
little creation.
Grow deeper and deeper,
and touch the sublime.
Draw closer and closer,
get lost in amazement,
and feast on wonder.
Open your perceptions
and join the party.
We are dancing together,
in the circle of
my throbbing, drumming Cosmos.

The creations of the Field are produced over billions of years, through trial and error. With living organisms, the successes are noted and stored in the DNA like a memory bank, so that they can be replicated and built on. There is an observable, slow style that might be called "incremental creation." Usually, though not always, systems are built up slowly, from pieces added and worked into existing realities over time. Occasionally, there are leaps or quantum jumps in the pace of creation, but this is rare.

The painstaking mode of creation produces complex systems that are woven tightly, intricately together. Integration of parts is total. Every part plays its individual role in sustaining the system as a whole. But there is more going on in the Field's systems than integration, no matter how complete. The systems possess a dynamic of self- balancing. Either within organisms or through the interaction of separate parts of the system, self-balancing mechanisms interact to sustain and preserve the functioning of the system as a whole. This is a fundamental characteristic of creations of the Field.

Another way of saying the same thing is that the Field nurtures its creations by building in intricate balancing mechanisms that operate to protect the integrity of its systems as a whole. In this self-balancing, protective, adaptive process, the thrust appears to be to protect, sustain and expand life. The systems have an organizational elegance, an intelligent fitting together and working together to sustain the system as a whole. This is a hallmark of the creations of the Field.

For example, over the past 4 billion years the temperature of the sun has gone up dramatically. It is now some 25% hotter than it was four billion years ago when Earth was formed. Throughout that time, and until today, the temperature on Earth has remained constant. Earth has responded adaptively to keep conditions on its surface hospitable to life. One prime way that it has done that is by pulling carbon dioxide out of the atmosphere. Carbon dioxide traps heat from the sun. Less carbon dioxide in the air means lower temperatures on Earth. Earlier, there was 1,000 times as much carbon dioxide in the air as there is now. This trick has been accomplished primarily by pulling carbon dioxide into marine creatures, trapping it in their shells, and then sinking them to the bottom of the ocean when they die. This is a brilliant adaptation, a brilliant solution to the problem posed by rising sun temperatures.

In a similar process, the polar icecaps also regulate temperature, in a cycle that recurs about every 100,000 years. When the icecaps expand, they reflect more light and heat away from the earth, and temperatures in the atmosphere drop. When they contract, as they are now doing, they reflect less light and heat away, and temperatures rise.

Similar mechanisms of balance are observable in nature. It is a recent realization that predator-prey relationships in the natural world are subject to adjustments. Without wolves to keep their numbers trimmed, the elk and deer populations burgeon, the plants begin to suffer, and the system threatens to go into disequilibrium. In the absence of human intervention, the numbers of wolves and the numbers of elk and deer adjust themselves through their interaction. If there are not enough elk to feed the wolves, the wolf population diminishes, and the elk population starts to go back up. If there are too many elk, the wolf population goes up and diminishes their numbers. Similar balancing mechanisms operate all over the natural world, operating to sustain and harmonize and protect the system as a whole. It is a nurturing function of Being, built in as an integral part of the system as it was put together. It is an interesting aside that human beings and their activities and decisions are now being regarded as an embodiment of the regulating, balancing processes. We are most aware these days of the ways in which the human community is destabilizing nature, and this is of very great concern. However, the very bringing to bear of our reason and judgment on the problems caused by our mistakes is perhaps part of the regulatory process. It is the human, after all, who is acting to reintroduce wolves into the ecology of the wild spaces. This is a balancing move. Being is moving the pieces, through us, to protect the system as a whole.

In human and other mammalian bodies, there are countless processes that rely on systemic regulation to keep the organism in equilibrium. Human and animal life would not even be possible without these regulatory processes. Blood pressure falls into this category, as well as blood clotting, which is a response by the system to a break in the arterial system. The hypothalamus controls body temperature, and induces shivering to increase body temperature when it falls to the lower parameters. The blood PH is being constantly rebalanced to keep it in a zone healthy for the blood cells. There are also balancing mechanisms operating in the human gut to keep the system in trim.

James Lovelock unsettled the scientific world recently by proclaiming the earth to be a vast, self-balancing super-organism that actively modifies the planetary environment to produce the environmental conditions necessary for its own survival. This is his Gaia hypothesis. It was a giant step away from the Newtonian/ Cartesian mechanistic worldview. Predictably, the old scientific guard ridiculed the vision, but people across the world immediately incorporated it into their possibilities for reality. It is a vision that looks to the future of human consciousness, to what we may become after a little more evolution, rather than to the past.

The balancing mechanisms of the Field's creations are treated by the scientific establishment as mechanical operations. In this view, the creative source of the systems is the systems themselves, and they consist largely of feedback loops. The systems, which are regarded as arrangements of discrete, separate pieces, have somehow figured out how to create miraculous mechanisms to sustain themselves. It seems hard at this point to maintain an allegiance to the old view. It is like asserting that monkeys playing in a junkyard would eventually build a 747.

One alternative is to view the balancing functions as the intelligent and beautiful creations of the Field, itself a living and creative intelligence. If the Field has created the universe that we live in, it can certainly take steps to build in features that will preserve the beauty, stability and integrity of the system. The vast intelligence of the Field is at work here, and we are the beneficiaries. It is working on our behalf.

16

Destruction

Old age on one shoulder,
death on the other.
Together, we three
march toward
an uncertain destination.

The Field not only creates. It also destroys. In the Hindu Vedanta of 3,500 years ago, three processes were outlined. These insights were anything but primitive. They were, in fact, characteristic of the Field.

First, there was Brahman, the fount of creativity. All things emerge forth into the world from Brahman. This is parallel to our view today that the material world, the explicate order, emerges from the unmanifest, implicate order, the quantum Field.

Second, there was Vishnu, the sustainer. Vishnu holds material reality together. He is the process that sustains life and is the moving force behind all of life's processes. In our modern world, scientists are still fervently examining reality to find the equivalent of Vishnu, to understand the forces that hold material reality together. This search has identified four forces at work in the universe: gravity, the electro-magnetic force, the strong force, and the weak interaction. Altogether, they amount to Vishnu, the sustainer, who keeps the world in place and going.

Finally, there is Shiva, the destroyer. Shiva's job is to take material reality apart. He is constantly at work in the universe, removing items for existence, from cells to humans to planets and stars. Sometimes he does his job with incredible violence.

The ancient Hindus couched their insights in vivid anthropomorphic imagery. The three processes were embodied by giant, powerful gods, and a great body of literature was created around the exploits of these gods. The insights were passed through the Mithal, the realm of pure imagery, and turned into images, symbols and metaphors. This imagery was useful for the understanding and worship practices of the common people. Too often, we in the West have taken the Indian pantheon of gods to be a limited and primitive belief system. This is not the case. A serious look at Hinduism reveals that, beneath the vivid iconography, the brilliant thinkers of that time were examining the nature of the cosmos just as our scientists are doing today. They expressed the processes that they saw operating in terms of symbol and metaphor, which was the primary teaching mode, the means of passing on information and insight for millennia before modern times. In our time, we have moved from metaphor to linear rationality to convey our insights. Both are effective means. We have to have a deep respect for those ancient Indian thinkers when we see the depth of their investigation into the nature of reality.

The process of destruction in the system is scary. Most of the time, we avoid the subject until it is placed squarely in front of us by our experience. However, it is an integral part of reality, of the way that the Field unfolds the material realm. Every material object, animate or inanimate, that emerges from the ocean of wave/particles is destined to return to that ocean. Only the Field endures. Its creations are impermanent and transient, all of them. The explicate world is temporary. Only the implicate world of pure potential is eternal.

In the macro world of the universe, destruction plays itself out in vivid, cataclysmic ways. When a star some twenty times larger than our sun pulls gases and particles together and begins to burn, hydrogen atoms fuse to form helium nuclei. Temperatures reach 10 million degrees. Light and energy are released. The star will burn hydrogen for around 10 million years or so, changing hydrogen into helium. Finally, the hydrogen available to the star is used up. The star implodes and its temperatures reach 100 million degrees. Then the helium starts to burn, forming carbon. When the helium is exhausted it compacts down into just carbon that is in fact a massive diamond. It is called a white dwarf. Its temperature reaches millions of degrees of heat.

If large enough, the star crushes the carbon diamond, and the carbon begins to burn. It burns for about a thousand years, producing oxygen. Then the carbon in turn is used up, creating silicon. The silicon burns for only about a week, creating iron. The iron won't burn because it takes in more energy than it releases. The star's temperature goes to around 10 billion degrees, making the protons so agitated that they collapse the structure of the star. The star cannot survive any longer. In a space of two seconds, the star collapses to a tiny point. Every atom and every particle is destroyed. The protons and electrons are fused together to form neutrons. This produces a pulsar or neutron star. The work of 10 million years is eliminated in two seconds. Shiva has arrived. This happens in our Milky Way galaxy about once a century. Throughout the universe it is happening continuously. Destruction is built into the nature of reality.

Our life unfolds in the midst of death. It is all around us. It is integral to the system. Death and destruction are necessary to the unfolding of the Field. New patterns of reality can only appear if the old and worn-out pieces of life are cleared away. The arrival of the new and fresh depends on this process. If we can assimilate the Field as our reality, and embrace all aspects of it, including death and destruction, perhaps we can face our own prospects with less fear. Perhaps we can live our lives with a larger awareness, and be grateful to participate, however briefly, in the miraculous pageant that is this life.

17

Orientation

I sit in myself,
yearning,
incomplete,
longing for something
that I cannot even express.
I turn that longing
toward the world.
I grab and claw
to fill the emptiness,
but nothing satisfies.
Then,
in grace,
I deepen,
And Vastness
fills my emptiness.
I am filled with
living, mysterious substance.
It was there all along.
The empty hole
was waiting for it,
demanding it,
and pushing me toward it.
At this moment,
I am complete.

Humans are adaptable creatures. They can arrange themselves in any number of ways, both as individuals and in groups. The mode of arrangement that we choose depends entirely on our orientation.

Orientation is fundamental to functioning. Without basic orientation—knowing who we are, where we are, and what surrounds us—we are helpless and inoperative. We are in the position of an autistic child. In order to operate in the world and in our life, we must have a North Star to orient toward. The North Star that we choose affects everything. It determines our identity, or who we take ourselves to be. It determines our values, or what we consider to be important. It determines our behavior and goals, or where we are trying to go with our efforts. The North Star that we choose orchestrates, organizes and fuels the entire life process.

In this culture, our North Star is consumerism and materialism. In pursuit of the good life, Americans have come to believe that it consists of accumulating money and things. Perhaps as a reaction to the deprivation experiences of our immigrant population, having material goods has risen to the top of the list of priorities. The burgeoning industrial society, with its mass production methods and lower prices, has put most goods within the reach of the common people. We are all eager to have one of everything. We believe that having things will result in fulfillment and lasting happiness. We continue to believe this, even though our experience shows us that the joy of having something new, even something that we have longed for, is transient and short-lived. It does not solve the problem.

The impulse toward consumerism as the key to fulfillment is, of course, fueled by the advertising industry. It is heartily endorsed by the cultural complex in general. It is apt and laughable that, in the midst of the nationwide shock and grief of 9/11, President Bush's response to the nation was to urge everyone to go shopping. How have we come to this? How have we allowed our lives to become so superficial and pointless? How have we succumbed to the need to have all the latest gadgets while a substantial number of people in our own society and across the world do not have the basics of a decent life—food, water, housing and medical care? How have we gotten so seriously off the road? Are we irretrievably decadent? And, what can be done now?

One possibility that might help would be to re-orient ourselves to the Field as our North Star. If we turn our attention even briefly to the miraculous nature of life and creation, we still have the capacity to be struck with wonder. We are currently in a state of sleep, mesmerized by the neurotic, consumerist conclusions of the cultural complex.

However, forces are at work to wake us up. Foremost among them is the desolate emptiness produced by this way of life. Enough of us are having the experience of empty despair that the society as a whole is beginning to realize that something is very wrong. We are looking desperately for some kind of meaning, some other road to take, some solution for the conditioned misery produced by the consumerist answer to life. This uneasy discontent is fertile ground for evolution.

Turning to the Field as the North Star might produce a wealth of positive results. Perceiving the unfolding of the cosmos, from the Big Bang to the present, generates a response of awe and wonder. A sense of sacredness cannot be far behind. Although we have desacralized our lives and our world, the realities of the Field's creative, sustaining and destroying capacities are still operating right before our eyes. The universe is no less miraculous now than it has been for the past 13.7 billion years. Societies before us have oriented themselves to the Field as their North Star. Each in their own way and with their own images, they put the livingness of the Field in central place and instructed their children about it. Most of those societies we would call primitive, but which is the more primitive society—the one that puts unseen, dynamic, unfolding, creative reality as its North Star, or the one that is miserable, lost in its toys and diversions?

The Field is available as a solution, or at least as a direction. Besides re-sacralization, focusing on the Field also encourages a community of equality. With all of creation as its product, and unity as its nature, it undergirds and supports the evolution toward a new human consciousness. It is consistent with less greed, less personal aggrandizement at the expense of the group, and a greater sense of responsibility toward the whole functioning system. Our attitudes could change, not only toward our fellow humans, but also toward other species and the whole natural world. We might begin to take better care of the planet and its other inhabitants. With the Field as a new North Star, we might be able to view ourselves appropriately and realistically within reality as a whole. We might actually be able to see ourselves in context. A new day might begin to open up.

18

Recurrent Creation

With great awareness,
enter the fertile space,
alive with possibility
and teeming with life.
Surrender the mundane,
drop into a well.
Let gratitude trump fear,
and walk into eternity.

Our view of reality is shifting. The assumptions we hold are changing. Mainstream science was constructed on a particular worldview that has now been challenged and is eroding. That worldview included considering the universe as occupying a static, stable and unchanging space, and time as a linear, measurable unfolding of events. It also included the assumption that the universe was created at one moment in time and proceeded in a linear fashion through an evolutionary process, culminating in our present time.

Einstein's relativity theory overturned the old views of time and space. It turns out that both are relative, meaning changeable, rather than absolute, or unchanging. They present themselves for perception and measurement in different ways, depending on the circumstances surrounding them.

There is an alternative way of looking at the creation of the universe. It was articulated in the 12th century by the Sufi mystic, Ibn Arabi. He called his idea "Recurrent Creation." It states that the universe is being re-formed every nano-second, in bursts of creativity.

In this view, the entire cosmos, in all of its infinite complexity and size, is wholly re-created by Being at every moment. These re-creations are so rapid and follow each other so closely that they are not separately perceptible to us. We perceive a continuous, stable world when the reality is really a series of separate worlds, each following the previous, and appearing in sequence so rapidly that they blend together to produce the illusion of continuity. It is rather like the experience of sitting in a movie theatre. Although we know that the film projected on the screen is coming from a stream of separate, individual image frames on the film-strip, the illusion on the screen is one of continuity and normal life. The illusion takes over, and, while we are under its spell, we believe it completely. Our disbelief is suspended. The illusion is completely compelling.

Another useful metaphor is a strobe-light. The cosmos is being created and projected out in flashes, like the flashes of a strobe. In our experience, we meld the individual flashes into a seam-less continuity, a linear unfolding that appears to our perception. Another part of Ibn Arabi's idea is that each successive re-creation is very slightly different. Reality comes through a kind of tem-plate, which changes ever so slightly with each re-creation. The net result is that billions of re-creations, each through a slightly shifting template, gives us the impression of seamless continuity, that someone is, for example, walking across the room, that life is unbroken and linear.

A number of corollaries flow from Ibn Arabi's idea. One is that the universe and all of creation are always fresh, just presently created, always new. In this system, life can never be stale. This fits with our experience. We appear to live in an ocean of ever-fresh livingness, fertile and forever renewing itself. If the world is being created anew in every micro-second, such a fresh world would be the result.

Quantum physics is currently considering several possibilities that are as radical as recurrent creation. One is coming out of the discovery that the act of observation is an integral part of the outcome of an experiment. Researchers discovered that if they expected to find a particle in light, they found a discrete, material particle. If they expected to find a wave in that same light, they found a wave, immaterial and invisible. Light appears to fluctuate back and forth from particle to wave, according to the expectations of the observer. Quantum physicists talk about the wave-form "collapsing" into the particle form on observation. The wave-form is unmanifest. It does not exist at any particular site in space. It exists across a range of locations, distributed over an indeterminate space as a wave-form. When it collapses into a particle, the particle becomes material form in a particular place.

This discovery has led to speculation that our world is a function of our consciousness, that it does not collapse into material being until we turn our attention to it. It exists in wave-form, in potential and unmanifest, until it is touched by consciousness and attention. This is a really radical idea. By comparison, recurrent creation seems rather mild.

We are in a time period when reality is being re-defined. The certainties that we had about what is real, how reality is structured, what is actually there and how it functions, are disappearing. It is impossible to predict where this new thought will lead. The only thing that is certain is that our previous conceptions of reality were too small. We know less than we thought we knew, and the cosmos is infinitely more complex than we thought. Hang onto your hat. It is going to be an interesting ride.

19

The Radiant Fog

You can locate me,
everywhere.
I am totally alive,
everywhere.
My qualities reside,
everywhere,
My intelligence is active,
everywhere.
My presence can be felt,
everywhere.
The center of my heart
is here and now,
and everywhere and forever.

The Field is a cosmos-sized, invisible, alive and aware, force-field. It can be pictured as a radiant fog. This is only one way of attempting to grasp it with images. Other possibilities exist. It could be envisioned as a mammoth electro-magnetic field, with forces operating that are conducive to the creation and the sustaining of life. The exact image is not important. Grasping its nature is the point.

By definition, a field is equally located at every point within itself. Its nature is homogeneous throughout. If we choose to focus on the Field as sub-atomic particles emerging from nothingness and disappearing back into space, then this process is the crucial process occurring throughout. If we choose to regard living, intelligent Being as its basic nature, we can see it as a living matrix of mind, spread across the cosmos, out of which emerges the three-dimensional realm that we live in.

The point here is that every point in the Field possesses the same miraculous nature and qualities, both the three-dimensional, material forms and the space around and between them. All of it, forms and space, are emerging out of the ground of living, non-manifest Being. It is possible to talk of the ground as an energy field, but this leaves out crucial aspects. An energy field can be understood in the context of the old, dying Cartesian/Newtonian framework, as a lifeless, mindless, mechanical phenomenon of nature. The Field of Being is the antithesis of this. It is not only aware and intelligent. It is the very principle of intelligence itself. Much closer to the truth is the view that has surfaced at various times in the past, that of considering the universe as mind, as cosmic consciousness. This view was the basis of Richard Bucke's 1905 book, *Cosmic Consciousness.* Written before any of the discoveries of quantum physics were made, it is still worth reading as an alternative to the mindless, soul-less, mechanical Cartesian/Newtonian worldview that is now disappearing. Viewing the cosmos as mind is compatible in every way with the new structure of consciousness that is emerging in our time. It is compatible with the new discoveries of quantum physics, with the singularity of the unified field and the realization of absolute inter-connectedness of the web of life that we live in. Living at this time in history is like surfing a huge wave of immense power. We are propelled forward by immense forces that we do not and cannot fully comprehend, toward a future that we cannot envision because it is based on emerging givens that we have never yet experienced. The new structures are not yet fully in place. We are along for the ride, and propelled by the motive force of the wave, as the Field metamorphoses itself continually into new and previously unseen realities. We can only watch in fascination and wonder as the Field reconstitutes itself, and us, into undreamed-of possibilities.

20

The Apollonian and the Chthonian

Out of radiant sunlight,
the fecund dark unfolds.
In the luminous night,
my knowing disappears.
I surrender to mystery,
and I am swept
into the arms of the cosmos,
after a long time
away from home.

The Western reality system has been characterized as "Apollonian." It's a useful handle for a bundle of characteristics. The word derives, of course, from Apollo, the god of the sun. The Apollonian mind, familiar to us all because it is our own, is brilliantly sun-lit, clear and orderly. Reality is material, visible, simple, observable and apparent. There are no shadows, no darkness, no hidden, impenetrable mysteries. Humans are at the center of this reality. The universe is knowable and works reliably like a machine. It is unintelligent and exists, basically, on only one level of reality. Nature is controllable. Violence and terror are aberrations. Our safety and grasp of reality depend on understanding, classifying and ordering observable reality. We are at the center of things. Very little is alive in this universe, just a limited number of organisms, including ourselves. All the rest, all the material and space in the cosmos, is dead and inert. Everything is separate and stands apart from everything else. Very few things are connected to each other. Isolation and separation are the rule. There is reliance on the left brain and language to order experience. The view is reductionist and rational. There is a limited band of experience, and nothing is sacred. The Apollonian consciousness is the principal human strategy designed to lessen human anxiety. It creates the appearance of order and safety by screening out unacceptable, dark realities. It is based on denial.

The Chthonian consciousness is practically the polar opposite on every count. Chthonian means "from the bowels of the earth." It is a reality of shadowy, dark recesses, confused, unclear, chaotic, complex and only partially seeable. It is infinitely mysterious, full of incomprehensible forces at work. Reality is largely invisible and immaterial, and there are many levels of reality. The universe is a living organism, and nature is largely beyond our control. Humans are only one of the many organisms, all equally central to reality. The universe is basically unknowable. Violence and terror are an integral part of the cosmos, and classifications are useless because everything is completely unique. Everything is alive, in a reality that is vast, unlimited and irrational. The universe itself is intelligent, and is the source of all intelligence. Everything is connected in one vast, unified Being, and everything is sacred. The Chthonian is obviously with us from our primeval past. The Apollonian is the product of our recent history, the development of rationality and civilization. While the Apollonian is reductionist, and reduces reality to a narrow, sterile band of experience, The Chthonian involves the dark and mysterious, the uncontrollable and unknowable, subterranean forces and hidden sources.

The development of civilization is a progressive movement from Chthonian to Apollonian reality. The problem is that the Chthonian is the source of all meaning. No meaning resides or comes out of the Apollonian. It is analytical, basically pulling the cosmos and reality into its component parts. It does not synthesize the parts of reality into great wholes. In the process, depth is sacrificed to understanding. When Western culture lost its contact with Chthonian reality, it found itself in a de-sacralized world. Combining a worldview sucked dry of its depth and meaning with a definition of self as separate and unsupported accounts for the desolation and despair of the modern Western mind. We have unwittingly lost our roots. We are adrift in a meaningless universe. Somehow our development has led us to this cul-de-sac, to this dead-end of human evolution. This is our present situation.

We cannot go backward, so we must find a way to go forward that will yield greater cultural mental health. The issue is not to give up the Apollonian, but to balance it with the Chthonian. We must widen our screen to take in larger realities.

One possibility is to open to the cosmos as a living, intelligent and evolving Field, a Field that exists as the matrix out of which all material reality emerges. The story of the universe is the story of this Field. We are its latest brilliant innovation. Our consciousness is the Field's consciousness. the universe's consciousness, bending back on itself to reflect on its own accomplishments. If we are inside a mysterious and highly creative and evolving Field, and we are the creations of that Field, we have a means, by observing our own processes and development and particularly our consciousness, of connecting with and observing the Field itself. It only requires putting a new lens in place, crafting a new understanding of the nature of reality and our place in that reality. That is our present task.

21

Metamorphosis

A kaleidoscope of forms
swirls through time and space,
liquid, shifting forms,
molded and re-molded by life.
I am one of these forms,
thrown up by forces
too deep to know,
but not too deep to feel.
I awake to the miracle
of knowing that I know,
and I awake to the
silent, molding force
re-forming our world
eternally.

In slow motion, the Field is constantly shifting its shape. It is continually engaged in a process of metamorphosis, re-creating elements, dropping out elements, innovating, evolving itself, and emerging in new and startling ways. In these processes, the interaction of organisms with their environment shapes and reshapes them, calling forth new forms. We can see this everywhere. Think of a hummingbird's beak, perfectly adapted over time to reach deeply into the heart of flowers for their nectar. Think how different that is from the woodpecker's beak, designed to perfection to get at the tiny insects living in wood. Every organism is subject to these forces of adaptation. We are all being shaped by our experiences and interactions with the environment around us.

In this restless process, oppositional dynamics play a prime role. Countless patterns of interaction pit two organisms as adversaries. The interactions between the two are dynamic, that is, they cause things to happen to the organisms. The shaping process, the metamorphosis of the organisms, is triggered through their interactions. Through the miraculous capacities of the Field, both organisms are enhanced and further developed. We can see these effects clearly in the predator-prey relationships.

For example, the oppositional dynamic between the eagle and the rabbit offers a case study. The eagle possesses its attributes—sharp eyesight, powerful wings, speed, surprise, clutching claws, razor sharp beak—to enable it to fulfill its needs for food and energy. The rabbit has its own set of attributes—speed, nimbleness, a den to retreat into, good eyesight and hearing, and evasive, irregular ways of running to avoid capture.

In a direct, physical way, the eagle and the rabbit are both shaped by the dynamics of their interaction. The rabbit's gifts and talents for evasion sharpen the eagle's eyesight, speed, and capturing skills. The eagle's gifts and talents call forth sharper evasive skills in the rabbit's organism. The interaction between them is mutually beneficial to the further evolution of their species. Genetic development takes place, which is passed along by DNA to later representatives of their groups. A force of development takes place as they interact with each other. Metamorphosis and development are triggered by the experiences of life itself.

Here we are, of course, in the area that Charles Darwin famously researched and wrote about in *The Origin of Species*. Darwin's observations were astute and accurate, centering on natural selection and adaptation as the bases for evolution. What is missing today when we think of Darwin's evolution is a sense of wonder at the process. We somehow place the genius for evolution within the species themselves rather than within the Field. Evolution is metamorphosis. It is not just a slow, stately, mechanical change of characteristics over a long period of time. It is a genuine shape-shifting, a magical propensity endowed by the

Field itself. It is the capacity of the Field to alter physical reality. It is changing the givens in the physical world through the influence of a dynamic interplay. We should observe the process with wonder and awe. It is a purely magical power of the Field.

When we apply this to the human being, it becomes even more magical. Over eons, the Field has unfolded awareness in the human, moving from simple animal consciousness to human self-awareness. We are aware that we are aware. Over time, our pool of awareness has expanded exponentially, and is still doing so. We are aware now that we are the culmination, for the moment and as far as we know, of the 13.7 billion years of evolution of the universe. Our consciousness is the sudden and acute manifestation of possibilities latent in the Field since the origin. We are a study in the expansion, over time, of a talent for consciousness. We are the unfolding potential of the Field in the form of awareness.

The unfolding continues. Having created problems for the earth community with our gifts and our heedlessness, we are now turning toward the application of our gifts to try to find solutions to the problems. That is the universe, the Field, turning toward itself to redress an imbalance in itself. We happen to be the means employed. Whether or not we can solve the problems remains problematical.

Our struggles with our self-created problems are a new case-study in oppositional dynamics. Faced with a formidable adversary, in the form of the natural consequences of our mistakes, perhaps the dynamics of that opposition will evolve us. The struggles with our opposition, the troubles in the environment, may call evolution forth out of us. Problems can generate growth and change. Perhaps our current problems will pull new and unsuspected qualities out of us, qualities latent and hidden until now, called out by the threatening environment. Perhaps we contain the seeds of our own salvation, planted there at the origin by the Field, waiting to be enlivened by the Field and brought to manifestation. We can hope.

22

The Mithal

When I turned,
dear and familiar forms
had dissolved into
the morning mist.
Chimera.
Life.

Contrary to the American consensus view, which focuses on the material world as the only true reality, existence is a many-layered phenomenon. There are inner realms of non-material reality—a realm of light, a realm of energy, a realm of images—that are almost completely lost to modern consciousness because they do not exist in the consensus framework. Access to these non-manifest inner realms has atrophied, through lack of use, in modern man.

One of those inner realms is the Mithal, the realm of images. It was forcefully articulated by the 12th century Sufi mystic, Ibn Arabi. This realm is a rich storehouse of experience. Meaning is encoded directly into the symbols, archetypes, and images that live in this realm. This layer, the imaginal or mythological layer, is just as real as the material world but simply of a different order of reality. Images exist and have their life in it solely as images, without materiality. However, they are alive and dynamic. They appear in consciousness and cause things to happen in human minds and lives.

The images appear in consciousness wrapped in mystery. They operate on a different basis than the material world, a basis so deep in the Field that we cannot fully grasp it. This realm of imagery is accessible to us, but we must interact with it on its own terms, respectfully. It does not appear on demand. It comes both in dreams and in waking states, sometimes unbidden and almost always laden with deep meaning. It appears only as an act of grace. However, if we lay the groundwork properly, give it our full attention and wait respectfully, it will usually appear with its surprising depth and startling information.

Images from the Mithal are so woven into our life experience that we seldom notice them independently, unless they have a dramatic impact. Occasionally they arrive in consciousness with transformative information that shakes the whole system of the psyche. Jungian depth psychology has built its practice around attending to the images and their information. Jung realized that images are the language of the unconscious mind and the language of the soul. Jungian practice today follows the imagery of dreams closely to observe the unfolding of the soul and the interface of that unfolding with life's dilemmas.

Jung deeply investigated the role of imagery in his own psyche. He had extensive conversations at the inner level with Philamon, a long-bearded, fancifully dressed, Pagan entity. Over a period of years, his interactions with Philamon yielded great results. Jung credited Philamon as the source of many of his deepest insights into the human psyche. In a sense, he owed his career and his stature in the field to Philamon. At a minimum, his experience with Philamon was formative and seminal. Jungian work today makes use of imagery in a form called "active imagination."

Ibn Arabi had a similar experience nine centuries earlier. Arabi was the greatest philosopher of his age. He wrote something like 400 books, and is still revered today as "the Great Sheikh" or "the Great Teacher."

Ibn Arabi reported that, in his imagination, he walked around the Ka'aba in Mecca with Sophia, the goddess of wisdom. Sophia took the image of a beautiful young girl. As they walked around and around the Ka'aba, they had long, involved conversations about the nature of reality. Arabi credited these interactions with

Sophia, as Jung credited his with Philamon, as the source of much of his insight.

In the modern world, Tibetan Buddhism has the most sophisticated use of images. A central practice in this belief system involves bringing up deities in the mind's eye and inter-acting with them. The Tibetan iconography is extremely rich, and the deities are visualized not just by themselves but in context, with individual palaces, consorts, attendants and attached minor deities included. Behind this exotic use of the imagination is a deep and skillful transformative intent. Each deity represents a quality that the devotee is reaching for and needs to apply in his own life—strength, peace, will, compassion, clarity, etc. By visually communing with the deity who embodies this quality, the devotee absorbs some of the quality for his own use. When the visualization/absorption practice is finished, the deity is dissolved. The Tibetan practice is based on the belief that our minds are the source of our experience. It is a powerful and skillful use of the Mithal.

Einstein used imagery in the Mithal to work out his theory of the relativity of time and space, as did Friedrich Kekule in arriving at the molecular structure of benzene. All innovation, in fact, scientific and otherwise, begins with images of the thing being brought into manifestion. It moves through that level before entering the world of forms.

Joseph Campbell said that there are two periods in life when the imaginal realm is most important. The first is the period from 4-12 years old, when the images and archetypes of mythology teach the young person what and how to be, what to grow into. The second important period is in older people, when mythology and deep imagery appear to carry the person through the last phase of life and out the last door, the "grand egress."

Older people, who have done the hectic outer life, with its focus on family, children, career, success, relationship and material well-being, naturally and increasingly turn their focus from the outer world to the inner realms. Jung said that, as we age, we naturally withdraw from life and slow down somewhat. This creates excess libido that goes into the inner realms, into the Mithal and into mythology. This reorientation requires less energy and more contemplation, and yields more depth, richness and meaning. Older people, growing progressively less interested in achievement, begin to look intently at their lives for meaning because they are trying to make sense of what they have experienced. So, it is a natural thing to turn to the inner, imaginal realm, where that meaning resides.

Our culture has an unhealthy relationship with images. On the one hand, their power is recognized by the advertising industry and turned toward manipulation. So, we are inundated with a cascade of images in our daily life, many of which are devoted to stimulating consumerism. On the other hand, the culture denigrates the importance of the imagination, considering inner experience to be baseless, unimportant fantasy and hallucination. It can only be this way in a culture that is overwhelmingly materialistic. Non-material realms such as the Mithal are summarily dismissed. There is no recognition that the Mithal is a powerful, creative and generative part of reality, that it plays a central role in the evolution of consciousness. Though we use it constantly to our benefit in our life experience, we do not acknowledge its power and importance. The Mithal and its imagery are a central and mysterious element in the realities of the Field. Perhaps we are growing toward a time when our perceptions will make a place for this deeper truth.

23

Symbols and the Mithal

Every day is the first day.
Every breath is the first breath.
Every thought is the first thought.
It is always now.
We dance the dance
of perpetual Presence
and celebration.
The whole unfolding of the Cosmos
is brought forward
into every moment.

One of the most mysterious and generative parts of the Mithal and the Field is the symbol. A symbol is an image that carries meaning. It must be distinguished from an ordinary image in consciousness. It is special.

Our mental functioning is a steady stream of images, day and night. The images succeed each other, each following on the other, like pearls on a string. Our mind is rarely quiet, without imagery. The mind-stream is incessant, sometimes relentless. We are intimately familiar with images moving through our mind.

Ordinarily, our mind works with signs. Sign is a term of art. It signifies an experience where one image stands for and represents another. For instance, the cross is universally recognized to stand for Christianity. Signs are simple equivalents, a kind of shorthand reference. They are the ordinary way our mind works to order and understand our experience. They are not symbols.

Occasionally, however, an image appears that has a special quality, completely unlike the other images. It is numinous, lit up. It seems special and mysterious and potent. It is compelling and luminous. It has some kind of strange, magnetic, attractive power that demands our attention and interest. It has the power to sustain itself, becoming part of our consciousness for days, and occasionally for a lifetime. This is the symbol. It can come during either waking or sleeping, but it is particularly associated with dreaming. Jungian psychology pays close attention to dreams and their symbols, searching in them for developments in the organism that are beyond the conscious mind. Symbols are images that carry deep and occasionally profound meaning, although we may, at the moment, have no notion of what that meaning might be. If we note it and give it some attention, we may be able to parse out the meaning. It may, however, be complex, and difficult or impossible to unravel. Meaning is encoded into the symbol, into the very interstices of the visual image. And, the symbol may mean more than one thing. Symbols possess the uncanny power to embody multiple meanings simultaneously, all of them equally true. The surface meaning, the first meaning discerned, may be only a covering for more information at deeper levels.

Science now distinguishes man from the animals by calling him the "symbol-making animal." No other animal is thought to possess this ability. Formerly, science considered man to be the "tool-making animal." Then, it was discovered that chimpanzees use long blades of grass to stick down into termite mounds and pull up a snack. Since the practice was clearly a use of tools, the scientists had to find another definition of man to distinguish his uniqueness.

The origin of symbols is shadowed and mysterious. They reside deep in the Mithal, and deep within the Field. They appear at their own leisure. A true symbol rises up of its own accord. It cannot be conjured up on demand. Symbols are, in a sense, acts of grace. When they arrive in consciousness, they come trailing intimations of a deeper, unseen order of reality. They also track the individual's personal evolution, the evolution of the soul. They carry a sense of profound truth, a glimpse of deep truth beyond the chaos of street consciousness.

Symbols are deeply personal. The information that they encode usually relates only to the individual receiving the symbol. It arises out of their personal history. Dictionaries of symbols and their respective meanings are useless, because the same image as a symbol can mean very different things to different people, depending on their experience. Occasionally, however, a powerful symbol may move out and affect the wider culture. The death of Princess Diana is an example. She functioned as a symbol to many people, probably for many different reasons, and her death impacted individuals all across the world. At the cultural level, symbols can be an extremely potent force. The mythical symbols of the Teutonic gods and the Aryan Superman were powerfully used by Hitler to bind the German people together to follow his program.

Symbols sometimes constellate, or cluster. In this phenomenon, an evoked symbol is joined by a second, somehow linked and connected to the first. Then, a third and fourth may arrive and join the group, until the person has an aggregation of symbols grouped together, all inter-related, all full of information. Each member of the group will hold a different facet of the truth of the information. Altogether, the cluster is formidable.

It can carry a great deal of information, and can be redolent with depth and meaning. Much fine literature appears to arise out of the clustering of symbols. Mystical schools may arise out of this process, as well as business enterprises and the establishment of other institutions.

Our interaction with symbols can add dimensions to our lives. Arriving from the Mithal and the Field, another realm of reality, they appear like a traveler from a distant land, capable of energizing and expanding our possibilities. Since we cannot call them up on demand, our job is to wait expectantly, like a "cat at the mouse-hole," and recognize them when they appear. They are a gift.

They can arise from anywhere. They can be triggered by the title of a book in a bookstore, a chance remark of a friend, or an item in the morning newspaper. They can be recognized by a sudden tiny jolt to the system, a sudden sense of alertness that we need to slow down for a moment and attend closely to this experience. They arrive, announcing themselves by compelling attention in a special way. They have much to reveal to us, but to receive their gifts we must pay close attention. As the Jungians have stated, they can represent signposts in the unfolding of our personal evolution. They originate in the Field, and show up in our consciousness with the potential to bring real change. We should be aware of their power.

24

Archetypes and the Mithal

A silent pulse
that I cannot hear,
that I cannot see,
that I cannot touch,
courses through my body,
my mind,
and through the world.
Beyond my senses,
I know it is there,
and I sense it now,
in the deepest depths of my being.

Among the most important residents of the Mithal and the Field are archetypal images. They have been most recently explored and amplified by Carl Jung. They are dynamic images, held unconsciously, that form and impact our emotions, our ethical and mental outlook, our relationships with others, and thus our whole destiny. For our purposes, the Mithal and the unconscious mind are one and the same thing. In Jung's framework, the archetypes are held in the collective unconscious of the culture, which is parallel to being held in the Field.

The concept of a realm of supremely important and generative images goes back to the ancient Greeks, and specifically, to Plato. He postulated a non-material realm of perfect forms, a collection of ideas that formed the template for the material world and out of which the material world emerged. His idea of this ideal realm is very similar to Ibn Arabi's conception of the Mithal. Plato considered the realm of ideal forms to be more fundamental and more real than the material realm, because the material realm decays and vanishes, while the ideal realm is undisturbed and eternal.

Jung acknowledged his debt to Plato. Jung said: "Archetypes are active living dispositions, ideas in the Platonic sense, that perform and continually influence our thoughts and feelings and actions." He considered archetypes to be not just ideas or images, but biological entities, "living organisms, endowed with generative force."

This dynamism, or ability to make things happen, is the central characteristic of archetypes. In the Jungian framework, the archetypes are innate psychic structures, held as images of universals such as man, woman, mother, father, child, wife, husband, birth, death, etc. They are universal. They cross all cultural lines. They have the effect of pre-programming us, arising to affect our perceptions and behavior appropriately to the phase of life that we are currently in. In other words, they are patterns of human existence, a phylogenetic blueprint on whose basis our lives unfold through the various stages. They are models held in the Mithal that, when triggered, form us and shape us and tell us who and how we should be. They are primordial images of our possibilities and our unfolding as a human being. Archetypes are associated with and generate archetypal symbols, generally a cluster of visual symbols, with which they take their control over us and influence our consciousness.

Archetypes are latent in the consciousness until they are triggered, or "constellated," to use the Jungian language. They are hidden in a veil of potentiality and called forth by our experiences.

One example of archetypal constellation that can be observed often in our culture is the pre-pubescent young girl who goes through a radical change in appearance and behavior when the Siren archetype descends. From an energetic, fresh, enthusiastic, naïve and gregarious young child, the girl suddenly becomes a sultry, sexually provocative, teasing temptress, fully aware of her sexual power and determined to do everything possible to use it.

Her clothes change. She suddenly begins showing a lot of skin, and moving provocatively. He behavior changes radically. The child disappears, replaced by a facsimile of Marilyn Monroe. It is as if the child had poured herself into a vessel formed like Marilyn Monroe, and become that form, to the best of her ability. She is holding an inner picture, an image of herself merged with the image of Marilyn Monroe, and trying to match that image. The Siren archetype is very powerful and omnipresent in our culture. It is continually in front of us in our movies, TV and magazines. It is readily available for the child to absorb and emulate. When it is triggered, it will re-make the child, at least for the time that it is centrally active.

Other archetypes are operating in all of us, shaping our expectations, perceptions and dreams of ourselves. We can see the King archetype operating in corporate CEO's, as they try to project images of power and command at the top of the hierarchy. We can see the Hero archetype in our sports figures. None of us escapes the archetypal molding process. These primal images are fundamental to human life and human unfolding.

We know a great deal more about DNA than was available to Jung. If he had had access to that new knowledge, he might have agreed that the archetypal images are carried in the memory banks of the DNA and passed along to each new generation, along with an infinite amount of other information about the makeup of a human being. The DNA holds all of the experiences of human history. Jung said: "Ultimately, every individual life is the same as the eternal life of the species." There must be a means of transmitting this patterning through time and through genera-tions. The DNA is the vehicle that does that job.

From a higher perspective, the DNA is the tool used by the Field to shape the unfolding destiny of the human and other spe-cies. The Mithal, as the realm of dynamic images, is one level of reality within the Field. As it has done for the last 4 billion years on Earth, the Field is bringing its past successes into present play and building on them. It is folding back on itself and cumulating its creative breakthroughs and bringing them into the present. The DNA may also hold the seeds of the future. Our present knowledge of the genome accounts for less than 5% of the genetic material that we carry. That leaves 95% unaccounted for. We do not know the content of that other 95%. Is it possible that somewhere in that mysterious, unknown 95% of the DNA there are marching instructions for the future unfolding of humans?

We are protagonists in a gigantic macro-drama, orchestrated and progressively unfolded by the mystery that we call the Field. It is conceivable that, having been endowed with the new capacities of self-awareness, language and symbols, we will enliven the drama, speed up its unfolding dramatic arc, and usher in a new act.

25

The Constructed Self

Stumbling on a dark road,
looking for guidance,
filled with anguish,
hoping for the dawn.
I lift my head,
I focus my sight,
I open my cells,
to a radiance that
I know is there,
but cannot see.

Because the culture is fixated on the surface of reality, we have to construct a self during our childhood. The true self, the essential self, is not acknowledged. There is no place for it in the Western framework, and so it recedes into the background. It can be recovered later in life, but it requires a great deal of serious work to do so.

The growing child constructs a self, a false self, slowly, by putting together bits and pieces of data. Interaction with the parents provides data about their preferences for the child's development, the way that they want him or her to be. The child has to decide how to respond to these molding pressures. Some children acquiesce, and try to become a self that is as close to their parents' wishes as possible. Others rebel against the program, struggling with the parents from the beginning and determined not to follow the program. The choice made by the child at this juncture goes with him or her through later life, and becomes the basic posture toward life. Early interaction with the parents also affects the eventual adult worldview by generating conclusions about other people, the nature of authority and how to respond to it, conclusions about how much and who to trust. In the very formative period between birth and four, the child's psyche is still gelling. It is forming itself around its experiences, forming attitudes about trust, the nature of the world, and the nature of other people. The conclusions reached on these subjects then sink into the unconscious mind, and color every interaction with the world thereafter. This set of attitudes is a large part of the developing false self.

Slowly, and often painfully, the child constructs strategies, behavioral devices and defense mechanisms to deal with the world. Most of this work is done by trial and error. The child retains for later use those strategies that seem to work for it. The false self is put together piece by piece by conditioning. A personality is carpentered together to face the world. The organism is trying its very best to adapt to the circumstances in which it finds itself.

The strategies selected are always mechanical and repetitive, programmed and rigid. When the strategies and defenses swing into operation, the person will respond to given situations in fixed, inflexible ways. Often, the person attempts later in life to use strategies adopted at three or four years old. They rarely work well.

In constructing the false self, two principal experiences are created. The first is a sense of separateness. Every interaction with the community enhances the perception of separateness, and the child learns very early to perceive itself as separate from everyone else. This sense of separateness, in most cases, lays the groundwork for later feelings of isolation, alienation, and loneliness. Most adults have these experiences as part of their daily life, and they go through life coping with them as best they can. The current mind-set in our culture has separateness at its base. All our perceptions are filtered through the lens of separateness. It is the source of a great deal of human pain, and much dysfunction and trouble in the life of the community. Moving to Field consciousness is, by definition, moving beyond separateness. An awareness of oneself as a particle in the vast Field of Being lays the ground for experiences of connection rather than separation. If we can manage to move to Field consciousness, it would bring tangible benefits to our life.

The second experience of creating a false self is a sense of identity. This is a sense that you know who you are. You are aware of the unique composite of characteristics that distinguishes you from everyone else. This sense of identity is based primarily on image and memory. We hold a self-image in our mind. It is a composite self-image that coalesces all the diverse self-images that come out of memories, mental pictures of the face and body, interactions and experiences in life. The mind constantly reiterates and reinforces the false identity, based on these images. Characteristics that one considers to be oneself are all derived from memory. The spiritual problem is not that we have the wrong self-image. The problem is that our identity is based on empty images rather than something real, Being.

Because it is a construction, and is not based on anything powerful and real, the false self is always off-balance. It is always insecure, threatened, and fearful. It is reactive, defensive, and full of agitation. It is constantly trying to shore itself up by achievement and attention from others. Filled with a sense of lack of value, the response is to claw at the world to get value and support. The false self is always engaged in grasping for ground. Its basic problem is that it doesn't feel quite real. At some deep level, the false self knows that it is an empty construction resting on thin air rather than grounded in Being. It needs constant reassurance that it is here, that it exists as a reality in the universe, and that it has some importance, some place in the system.

It is also stale, based on old, static images. It brings forth memories of the past and superimposes them on the present moment. It has no ontological reality, and it knows it. If it could access Being, which is alive in the present moment and generating livingness, it could at last feel real.

The false self is an arrested development. It is also the result of our cultural characteristics, superficial and distorted. We know that we are evolving. Perhaps we are capable of growing beyond the limited confines of the false self. Moving to a realization that our true identity is a particle in the Field, and that we are as divine and have as much value as any other particle, we could begin to see that our sense of separation is unreality. However separate and isolated we may feel, it is indisputable that we are part and parcel of the mysterious Field.that is the universe. We only need to wake up to that fact, and make it a central part of our consciousness.

26

The Radiant Particle

I am bigger
than I dreamed.
I am broader
than I thought.
I am deeper
than I knew.
Radiance spreads
throughout the cosmos,
and I disappear
into it.

Our real identity, our true self, is a radiant particle in the Field of Being. The emphasis here is on singularity, the absence of separation. Our personal identity, including our name, personal history, personal wounds, triumphs and griefs, our hopes and fear and desires, are ephemeral, secondary and passing. The emphasis is on communion, oneness, identification with the Field. This is our basic identity.

There is no loss involved in giving up separateness. It involves moving closer to reality. Though it has fueled our development for millennia, perhaps since we came down out of the trees, it has now become an impediment to our further unfolding. The separateness imprinted on our nervous system is now the root of immense human suffering, in the form of isolation, alienation and despair. A posture of self-absorption is also at the base of the despoiling of our planet. If we honestly ask ourselves the question: "Where are we now?" the answer is: "we are lonely, desolate, alienated and in despair. Our planet is struggling to maintain itself in the face of our on-slaught and heedlessness. Our prospects, with our present mind-set and worldview, are very dim."

This is exactly the kind of impasse that the cosmos has, in the past, faced and resolved. Its style is a burst of hyper-evolution. In the early stages of life on the planet, the tiny organisms, in their success, began to manufacture so much oxygen that it threatened the existence of life on earth. Oxygen is a very volatile gas, and was toxic in large amounts to organisms on Earth. However, oxygen was the waste product of the successful life-forms, and it poured into the atmosphere in enormous, dangerous quantities. The concentration of oxygen threatened to halt everything. For some period of time, the future of life on Earth hung in the balance. The prospects did not look encouraging. It was a time when the entire Earth system was under the sword, just as it is now.

Then, a solution materialized out of the Field. Some life-forms miraculously learned to eat oxygen and use it for energy. The new fad spread rapidly. As they consumed it, the oxygen was taken out of the atmosphere, lowering its concentration to about 21%, optimal for life, where it has remained ever since. The Field found a way out of the oxygen dilemma, and life on Earth continued its development.

The moral of the story is that our salvation lies in evolution. We must now evolve in some haste. The source of evolution or metamorphosis is in the Field. It is its nature to be restlessly creative, to metamorphose, to generate and implement change in the material realm. And, it has a bias toward life. Time and again, in the unfolding of the universe, the Field has created conditions very delicately attuned to the emergence, continuity, and further development of life. For instance, the universe is now expanding at exactly the rate required to keep our world and our galaxy together. Any slower and we could not be here. Any faster and we could not be here. It is a primary talent of the Field to keep conditions within the parameters where life can flourish.

The Field is on our side in our efforts to continue to exist. Its bias is for life to flourish and complexify. The universe is not the empty, black, threatening and indifferent vastness that we have previously thought. Nor is it the kingly, micro-managing, puppet-master of religion's vision. It is simply the Field, vast, powerful, unfolding and evolving, metamorphosing, and endlessly creative. It has intelligence and consciousness, but it is nothing like the intelligence of humans. It is vastly deeper, so much so that when we get a tiny experience of its capacities we are electrified.

The powers of the Field should keep us in a permanent state of amazement and wonder. We exist every day in the midst of a gigantic light and magic show. It is shimmering around us in every moment, mysterious, stunningly beautiful, profound in its depth, and sustaining itself effortlessly for our inspection. It is endlessly creating and metamorphosing itself into new forms, while maintaining, in perfect balance and in a trillion ways, the existing system that it has unfolded up to this point. It is a great privilege to be alive within this Field. It is a great gift. The gift has been and continues to be bestowed upon us, but we have been too self-absorbed, too asleep, and too underdeveloped and immature to perceive it.

We must do our part in the evolution that is being forced upon us. The Field has so organized its sea of sub-atomic particles that it has created our forms and those of other species. In the subsequent endowment of consciousness, it selected us as the prime recipients of awareness. It continues to expand that awareness now in our crisis. In a real way, our responses to the problems facing us are the Field contemplating the Field. Human intelligence is now an important factor in Earth's evolution.

We can expect to see a process of trial and error employed, because that is its style. The outcome is uncertain. The continuance of the Earth experiment is in the balance. It is certain that we must act ourselves, to the best of our ability, to solve our dilemmas. We are the Field. We are its fingers and instrumentalities. We are the application of the Field, well-designed and adapted to the task, through which the problems will be dealt with. Intervention will not come from on high. It will come through us.

There are signs of unfolding evolution everywhere. At the very moment of our greatest, self-induced crisis, we seem to be waking up to new realities. These realities were there all along, over the 13.7 billion years of the universe and the 4 billion years of the Earth. We were not yet evolved enough to perceive them, however. Now, it appears that evolution is opening our eyes.

The realization of the Field as the primary reality carries with it a number of beneficial corollaries. With the living, intelligent and conscious Field as our worldview, we would no longer be miserably separate. We would no longer be fearfully unsupported. We could regain our rightful place in the universe. We could belong to this vast system. We could once again feel the holding of the Field of Being.

Awareness of the Field might also re-shape our greedy competitive, self-serving instincts. If every particle in the Field is equally divine and important, then every other person, species, and inanimate object has equal sanctity. Everything is sacred. Everything is derived from living particles, arranging themselves temporarily in form. It is all divine. It is all sacred. It is all worthy of our devotion.

If we could evolve in this direction quickly enough to save ourselves, perhaps we would find ourselves in a new realm, a re-enchanted universe compelling our wonder and admiration. Perhaps we could regain the sense of sacredness that we have presently lost and long to recapture.

The Field will assist us in this re-enchantment. It is its nature. It is always pushing in the direction of wholeness, health, and perfect integration of parts. It is our ally. It is our best hope. It is shaping its future evolution, even now, through us. We are quickly evolving into a new consciousness, Field consciousness, and it could possibly save us and our planet.